CLAIMING AN EDUCATION

CLAIMING AN EDUCATION
FEMINISM AND CANADIAN SCHOOLS

❧❧❧

Jane Gaskell

Arlene McLaren

Myra Novogrodsky

Canadian Cataloguing in Publication Data
Gaskell, Jane S. (Jane Stobo)
    Claiming an education: feminism and Canadian schools

(Our schools/our selves monograph series; 3)
ISBN 0-921908-02-4
ISBN 0-920059-86-4 text and trade

1. Sexism in education – Canada. 2. Educational equalization –
Canada. 3.Women – Education – Canada. 4. Feminism – Canada.
I. McLaren, Arlene Tigar. II. Novogrodsky, Myra. III. Our
Schools/Our Selves Education Foundation. IV. Title. V. Series.

LC212.83.C3G37 1989   370.19'345'0971   C89-095410-0

This book is published jointly by Our Schools/Our Selves
Education Foundation, 1698 Gerrard Street East, Toronto,
Ontario, M4L 2B2 and Garamond Press, 67A Portland Street,
Toronto, Ontario, M5V 2M9.

For subscribers to **Our Schools/Our Selves: a magazine for
Canadian education activists**, this is issue #7.

The subscription series Our Schools/Our Selves (ISSN 0840-
7339) is published 8 times a year. Second class mail registration
number 8010.

Design and art work by Goodness Graphics.
Managing Editor: Deborah Wise Harris
Printed in Canada by Del Charters Litho, Brampton, Ontario.

"The first thing I want to say to you who are students, is that you cannot afford to think of being here to receive an education; you will do much better to think of yourselves as being here to claim one. One of the dictionary definitions of the verb "to claim" is: to take as the rightful owner; to assert in the face of possible contradiction. "To receive" is to come into possession of; to act as the receptacle or container for; to accept as authoritative or true. The difference is that between acting and being acted-upon, and for women it can literally mean the difference between life and death."

Adrienne Rich 1977

This book is dedicated to our children:
Joanne, David, Jesse, Noah and Toby.

Table of Contents

Introduction

Since the late 1960's, the women's movement in Canada has identified, articulated and struggled around a variety of issues in relation to education. Education has had a relatively high profile for feminists, as it has for many social movements because it holds out hope for change among the young. But education has also seemed resistant to change, as it is so large, so multi-faceted, so closely tied to the local community, and at the same time protected at the centre from those who would have an impact.

In the late 60's and early 70's, however, there was a great deal of hope and optimism among women who wanted to change education. The job of making the problems visible was paramount at first. Teachers and students and parents had come to take gender inequalities for granted. Of course mothers in textbooks wore aprons and baked cookies. Of course little girls needed to be in separate playgrounds from little boys. Of course it was a good idea for a young woman to learn to type so that she could earn some money before she got married. What could possibly be wrong with that?

In striving to explain what was wrong with that, feminists had to educate educators in the ABCs of women's oppression. Assumptions which had been taken for granted about men and women were revealed as stereotypes. Differences between the sexes were shown to be inequalities. The "problem without a name", which Betty Friedan described so eloquently was identified, named, and analyzed. A new vision of women's place in the world meant re-examining everything that went on in schools.

Since that time, gains have clearly been made. Consciousness of the problems is much greater than it was. More women are going to law school; textbooks have been rewritten. Women's studies programmes exist. We have achieved employment equity legislation and an equal rights provision in the Charter of Rights. But the problems have not disappeared. The statistics on women's continuing inequality do not need to be reiterated here. Women continue to take most of the responsibility for unpaid work in the family. Women continue to get paid 60% of what men are paid. Violence against women persists.

What are we to do with these problems? How should we think about feminist priorities in today's schools? How do they link up with a broader agenda for educational change? The debates on such questions are intense and complex. Some would argue that women's problems have been addressed already, and that feminist issues must now take a back seat to the issues of racism, the rights of teachers or students and the core curriculum. Others disagree about the meaning of feminism, the issues and places where it makes sense to intervene, and the utility of specific remedial measures. None of the major questions are closed and none are easily resolved.

Moreover, any lingering belief that the schools might be changed quickly has disappeared. Free schools and deschooling no longer seem to be the radical, attractive alternatives they once did. Change, we now understand, involves the less glamorous day-to-day issues that every teacher, student and parent must confront. In a changed social and political context, we have to renew the enthusiasm and the clarity feminist educators had twenty years ago . It is time to rethink the feminist agenda in our schools, and to broadly examine its implications.

There is of course no one feminist, or even socialist feminist, agenda, and much of what is required for change consists of mechanisms for continuing debate and renewal. By reviewing our history, we can hope to learn from it and to clarify new areas of concern. The conclusion should not, however, be just a laundry list of feminist demands. Rather, it should be an understanding of the linkages among these demands, and between them and an overall agenda for change in schools.

For feminism means inserting the concerns of women from all walks of life into policy and practice, ultimately reshaping the whole so that it better serves both men and women. It is linked with the struggle to redress other inequalities, both as a matter of theory–because the persistence of one kind of inequality affects all forms of inequality; and as a matter of practice–because we need a coalition of all those who oppose that inequality. Examining the ways that social class, race, and culture are all gendered experiences helps us understand those issues. Examining the ways that differences among women are based in systematic inequalities of other kinds helps us understand the organization of women's experiences.

This book is organized into four chapters, reflecting four areas in which the women's movement has helped us rethink educational issues. The first chapter addresses the issue of equal opportunity, of how women have participated and achieved in the educational system, and how we can think about and tackle these inequalities. The second chapter deals with curriculum, in the broadest possible sense. It asks what is taught in schools, and how it is received by students. The third chapter deals with mothers, child care workers and teachers—those who do the educating, and who are most often women. It asks how we organize the provision of education, what that means for the lives of women, and how change might benefit students as well as educators. In the final chapter we pursue some of the above questions as they apply to post-secondary education and adult education, and we draw some general conclusions about the relationship between a socialist feminist politics and the issues we raise in this book.

The book has been written by three of us, and we have somewhat different concerns and backgrounds. Jane Gaskell teaches in the Faculty of Education at the University of British Columbia. Arlene McLaren teaches in the sociology department at Simon Fraser University. Myra Novogrodsky is coordinator of Women's and Labour Studies for the Toronto Board of Education, and currently teaches at City School in Toronto. Our experiences in the educational arena are varied, and include setting up women's studies courses and programmes at the levels of the school board, the university, and the ministry of education; organizing conferences, workshops and courses; and struggling with our own practice in classrooms, committees and collegial relationships. Our political backgrounds are also similar but different. Our experience in the women's movement goes from 1960's consciousness-raising groups to 1970's study groups, to 1980's committees and action groups. Our involvement in left politics goes from Marxist study groups to the Waffle to NDP organizing, with many stops in between for particular campaigns. Through it all we have learned from other women, from our families, our children, our friendships and our work. As feminism insists, "the personal is political," and our experiences as teachers, as mothers, as wives, as friends, and as white, middle-class activists, shape our analysis in this book.

We struggled to find one voice in which to write, even though first drafts never come out that way. We reworked each others' material, trying to incorporate the different strengths of each draft. In the end, we have decided to let the different styles and concerns that we bring to the writing appear at different points. We would like to thank George Martell for his commitment in seeing this project through, as well as Loren Lind and David Clandfield for their help with editing. Finding a balance between discussion of classroom practice and discussion of the research literature, between a focus on teachers' experience and a focus on policy issues, between an academic voice and a practical voice, is difficult. No one audience will find all they want here. Our plea is simply that these things are related, that educational research reflects political currents in the society, as does educational practice, that teachers' concerns as well as policy are shaped by the social organization of women's oppression and class and racial inequality. By pointing to some of the links, we hope to contribute to discussion of the whole. Ultimately, we hope that our discussion will inform political action, will help to renew enthusiasm, and will give clarity to the complex political struggles that lie ahead.

Chapter 1

Equality of Opportunity:
Issues of Access and Achievement

One of the earliest and most persistent demands of the women's movement has been for equal opportunity to achieve an education. Equal opportunity is a persuasive slogan for Canadians, because it invokes many true and noble ideals. It draws on the rhetoric of democracy, of liberalism and of the Enlightenment. It is something most people support.

Yet what is it? Is equal opportunity the right of a girl to take the same school courses as a boy? Or is it the chance for both girls and boys to advance according to the same standards? Does it mean attaching equal importance to courses in nursing and in engineering? Does it mean different courses for different students depending on their backgrounds and needs?

What equal opportunity has meant to women and to the women's movement has varied over time, depending on the political and economic context. Even at a single point in time, different parts of the women's movement have stressed different kinds of equality. This process of discovery and rediscovery, of changing demands but similar concerns, characterizes women's struggle for equality in education.

Some would argue that equality of opportunity is a liberal slogan that demands minimal change, that simply asks for women to be incorporated into existing social structures. As such, it would be quite possible to achieve, but not worth much. We resist this interpretation. We believe that any effort to truly incorporate women into educational institutions on the same basis as men would involve changing the structure of education. And this would mean changing the lives of both men and women for the better. Equality of opportunity, if it is seriously pursued, involves confronting the structure of gender inequality.

Early Struggles

To attend classes on an equal basis with men. Women wanted the right to study Latin with men, the right to go to medical school, the right to study with men at the same universities.

These were not trivial demands, and their fulfilment was not assured at the start. Even in Canadian public schools, which were co-educational from the beginning, the principle was often under attack. Egerton Ryerson, the first, and highly influential, superintendent of Ontario schools, was one who saw the exclusion of girls from grammar schools as a necessary step in the development of that province's education system. In 1865, he proposed to stop admitting girls to grammar schools and to the study of Latin. His ally, George Paxton Young, the grammar school inspector, argued the case this way: "There is a very considerable diversity between the mind of a girl and that of a boy; and it would be rash to conclude that, as a matter of course, the appliances which are best adapted for bringing the faculties of reflection and taste to their perfection in one must be the best also in the case of the other ... they (girls) are not studying Latin with any definite object. They have taken it up under pressure ... there is a danger of grown up girls suffering as respects the formation of their moral character, from attending school along with grown up boys". [1]

But Ryerson's and Young's arguments on this point did not prevail over the local school trustees, who accused the central officials of trying to take the schools back to the "dark ages".

Their interest, however, was largely economic. The impetus for co-education at that time was not sexual equality but financial stability. It was too expensive to provide separate schools for girls and boys. In order to have a public school with enough attendance to make it viable, it was necessary to enroll as many students as possible. Many schools settled for separate entrances and a wall down the playground to separate girls from boys.

Moreover, young women attended school more regularly than young men. Many children of both sexes avoided school throughout the 19th century; the boys to work in the fields, the girls to attend to domestic chores at home. But more young women than young men graduated from high school right up through 1950. British Columbia school reports show, for example, that 51% of high school graduates were women in 1880, 56% in 1890, and 63% in 1890. United States figures show a similar pattern. Sixty-five per cent of those who graduated from secondary schools in the US in 1890 were female. When the schools were open to women, women went to school.

The admission of women to higher education and professional training took more time and struggle.[2] Universities were considered "a male sphere, a place of serious learning that fitted men for positions in the public world. Women's entrance into the university was considered unnatural, both for the institution and for women. Higher education was considered at best irrelevant, and more likely detrimental, to women's future roles as wives and mothers."[3]

No medical school in Canada would admit women in the 1860's and mid-1870's, when Emily Howard Stowe and Jennie Trout decided to train as doctors. They went to the United States for their education and returned to fight for the admission of women to medical school here. As historian Alison Prentice and her co-authors put it, "Women had traditionally been healers, and caring for the sick was not a departure from woman's traditional sphere; but being highly educated to do so and being paid for it were."[4] In 1883, two separate women's colleges for medical education were established in Canada, affiliated with Queen's University and the University of Toronto. Others followed, slowly.

Access to legal education came later. After Clara Brett Martin was refused admission by the Law Society of Upper Canada in 1890, a bill was passed by the Ontario legislature to enable women to study law. Even after the bill was passed, the law society refused to put in place procedures for the admittance of women, until the premier of Ontario intervened. Martin became, in 1897, the first woman to become a full-fledged member of the legal profession and the first woman to practise law in the British Empire.[5] In Quebec, women were not allowed to practise law until 1941.

Women won formal equality by overcoming a great deal of prejudice and confronting entrenched male power. That was a giant step forward, but the fight for full equality in education only began with those battles. Since the public re-emergence of feminism in the late 1960's, women have argued that equal opportunity means a good deal more than equal access on a formal basis. The problems lie much deeper.

Probing The Roots Of Inequality

When educators began to re-examine the idea of equal educational opportunity in the 1960's, the issue arose not as a matter of gender but as a matter of social class and race. The United States "War on Poverty" drew attention to mass poverty in an increasingly wealthy society. The civil rights movement pointed to persistent racial inequality in a society that prided itself on its democratic and egalitarian ethos. The roots of these persistent inequalities seemed to be tied at least partly to problems in education.

How did education produce inequality? Not by excluding children from schools—for poor children and black children had the right to attend public schools by the 1960's—but rather, by failing to ensure that they all had the same chance to learn. They might all have a seat in the classroom, but some still achieved much less than others. Access was the same, but outcomes differed and the most disadvantaged at school seemed inevitably to be the children from poor and black families. Many large research studies showed that family background had a big impact on how well a child did in school. And how a child did in school had a strong impact on the child's later income and occupation. This research was used to argue for investing heavily in the education of disadvantaged students.[6]

Feminists used the same arguments to argue for better education for girls—who also seemed disadvantaged both at school and in the labour market. The evidence for women's disadvantage was threefold. First, women were less likely than men to go on to higher education, and university education was necessary for entry into higher paying jobs. In 1970, only a third of university students were women. Secondly, women earned much less than men. Full-time women wage earners earned 59% of what men earned in 1970. The disadvantage, and its link to education, seemed clear. Thirdly, girls and women took courses that did not lead to the highest paying and most prestigious sectors of the labour market. They were less likely to take industrial, mathematical and scientific courses. The 1970 *Status of Women Report* pointed out that one-quarter of all high school girls were enrolled in commercial courses leading primarily to secretarial jobs, compared with only 5% of boys. Seventy per cent of girls but 65% of boys were in academic courses, while 7% of girls were in "other" courses (mainly industrial) compared to 30% of boys. At the university level, 7% of the medical students were women and the report pointed out that "girls tend to concentrate in the faculties of arts and education."[7]

The Deficit Model

Once disadvantage is demonstrated, the question is how to explain it. Much of the explanation and thus much of the policy intervention in the 60's and 70's rested on the assumption that the disadvantage could be traced to some inadequacy in the children themselves. They came to school with a "deficit" that needed to be diagnosed and then remedied with good teaching. The deficit was usually traced to their home backgrounds. It might be wrong attitudes and values or inadequate skills and language. It might be lack of confidence or underdeveloped cognitive skills. The trick

11

was to spot the real trouble, and then intervene at school or preferably even earlier at daycare to make up the deficit.

This analysis led to massive intervention projects, like *Head Start* and *Follow Through* in the United States, aimed at boosting the school performance of poor children. These programmes were designed to teach poor children the skills and attitudes they needed at school but had not picked up in their homes as more privileged youngsters had. The assumption was that increased success in school would be translated into increased success in the labour market.

Many feminists adopted this dominant model to explain the disadvantage of girls in school. They suggested that girls similarly lacked some of the skills and personal attributes necessary for success, and that the school could make up the deficit. As a result, much of the research and the political struggle of feminists in the 1960's and 70's tried to pinpoint women's problems, and to suggest how schools could address them.

What were the deficits girls started with? A large literature on "sex differences" amounted to an attempt to explain what it was about women that led to their lack of achievement. Many suggested that little girls who learned to be quiet, to be feminine and to put other people's needs first would not become intellectually aggressive enough to excel at school. They were too passive, too interested in their social lives at the expense of academic achievement, too dependent, weak and quiet. As Anne Marie Henschel wrote at the time, "Girls are discouraged from growing into intellectually inquisitive, independent and self-assured persons. They are inhibited with regard to the acquisition of qualities that are highly valued in our society, and therefore are prevented from mastering the skills and achieving the status that would allow them to participate in the power structure". [8]

Obviously girls had been socialized in this way by a culture that fostered sex role stereotypes and by parents who subscribed to such stereotypes. But schools as well had a hand in reinforcing girls' inferiority. Schools were criticized for this and were called upon to change the situation.

Documenting the Deficit

There are many examples of research aimed at documenting the way stereotypes constrained achievement for women. Any number of characteristics of women could be held responsible for women's lack of success at school and work. Ability and aptitude, personality characteristics, family background and support, attitudes towards gender, and aspirations were all explored. Research on achievement motivation, on sex role attitudes and on brain lateralization and hormonal influence were all attempts to find out what it was that made women different from men, and what might explain their lower achievement. [9]

One popular explanation of why young women failed to pursue higher education was based on Matina Horner's research describing the "fear of success".[10] In her study, she gave students the following written cue: "At the end of first term finals, Anne was at the head of her medical school class".

Students were then asked to write about Anne. They proceeded to describe her as unfeminine, unattractive, and unlikely to succeed. They said things like, "Hard-working, devoted. Wears long skirts. Not feminine; tall, straight. Doesn't go out". One sketched this scenario: "Anne will deliberately lower her academic standing the next term while she does all she subtly can to help Carl (her boyfriend). His grades come up and Anne soon drops out of medical school. They marry and he goes on in school while she raises their family".

The same students were then asked to write about "John", who was also at the head of his medical school class. They described him as attractive, successful and very marriageable. Clearly men who are successful become more attractive, physically and socially, while women who are successful become less so.

Horner concluded that femininity and achievement are in conflict: "It is clear that a psychological barrier exists in otherwise achievement-motivated and able women that prevents them from exercising their rights and fulfilling their potential. Even when legal and educational barriers to achievement are removed, the motive to avoid success will continue to inhibit women from doing 'too well'–thereby risking the possibility of being socially rejected as 'unfeminine' or 'castrating'."[11]

Another particularly influential body of research asked why girls and young women have "low" and "traditional" aspirations. Why don't they want high-paying jobs? Why don't they want to stay in math and science? Why are they content with being wives and mothers? In short, what is wrong with them? A Labour Canada study of Canadian youth in 1986 concluded that "sex role stereotyping still appears to dominate the occupational aspirations of children and teens."[12] They found that even among the youngest of the research subjects, boys and girls gave significantly different responses to the items about the attractiveness of activities that involved responsibility, mechanical skills, and advanced education. Their family aspirations were equally stereotyped. "The girls tended to picture their adulthood as consisting of being mothers with small children and showed no awareness of the many years that women, even those who are mothers, do not have dependent children in their charge. The girls, almost without exception, expected to marry and have children. They seemed to assume without question that there would be a husband and father to provide for the family."[13]

Implicit here is the judgment that these young women are the cause of their own problems. They continue to aspire to traditional roles so they end up in them. If only they would change their aspirations and become more aware, they could get ahead, achieve more, become equal. In order to change their aspirations, and convince them they should want more than a home and children, what girls needed was more career counselling. They needed to learn to aspire towards non-traditional careers.

Biological explanations have also been popular in explaining why women avoid non-traditional subjects like science and math. In 1977, the Canadian Society for the Study of Education, for example, reprinted in its newsletter an excerpt from Richard Restak's research, suggesting, "Many differences between men and women are based on differences in brain functioning that are biologically inherent and unlikely to be modified by cultural factors alone...The male brain learns by manipulating its environment, yet the typical student is forced to sit still for long hours in the classroom...the classrooms in most of our nation's primary grades are geared to skills that come naturally to girls. Girls suffer later on, in crucial ways, taking scholarship tests that are geared for male performance." [14]

In such work, differences between the sexes are defined in fixed ways, based in biology, and used to justify educational policies that will further emphasize the differences.

Girls' lack of visual spatial abilities was also emphasized because of its purported relationship to mathematics and science. The debate about whether girls don't take mathematics courses because they do less well in them, or whether they do less well because they don't take mathematics courses, continues to rage in educational journals, and in teachers' newsletters.

This kind of "deficit" analysis calls for interventions which are remedial or which give information and advice to young women. A couple of examples illustrate the variety of responses that are possible, and the potential advantages and problems inherent in this approach.

The National Film Board produced a videotape called *I Want to be an Engineer,* which is designed to encourage young women to enter engineering. The film features three young Canadian women who are enjoying their careers in engineering. One is single, one a childless wife, and the other is a wife and a mother of four young children. All are "success stories", and the idea is to communicate to young women that they can do it too. Another such approach is *Careerscope,* a program developed at York University to "have role models demonstrate that women can be successful in careers that require math and science". The students were admonished not to drop subjects—such as math—that might narrow their career options. Films and panels of women from industry and government were used to show the advantages of careers in math and science. [15]

These interventions usefully counteract the stereotypes that women do not belong in engineering. They open up a sense of possibility for young women. However, the very rosy picture they paint takes attention away from the real difficulties—such as sexual harassment, discriminatory hiring and lower wages for women—that women do face in non-traditional careers.

Other interventions involve remedial teaching for girls. The EQUALS programme developed at the University of California developed tool-using workshops for girls, in order to give them the skills and the confidence they do not pick up in the home the way boys do. They also involved family members in a program called *family math*, a course to introduce math concepts and teach parents how to motivate and help their children with math at home. The idea is that anything to overcome the laissez-faire atmosphere at home, where boys are encouraged, and girls are ignored, will help girls.

Again, it's important to recognize that such interventions can be useful for some girls, who do learn to cope better with their science courses and develop confidence in their ability to do so. These interventions also draw attention to the lower participation of girls in math and science. At the same time, however, they suggest that the problem is located in girls' abilities and aspirations, instead of in the curriculum and instruction in math and science courses. They leave unchallenged the gender bias in the schools.

In summary, all of these remedial programmes rest on the deficit model. The basic assumption is that girls must be changed. Men are the model of achievement, and compared to men, women don't measure up. So it is assumed that women need remedial programmes to make them more like men. This leads to all sorts of interventions in the lives of girls to improve their attitudes and skills: assertiveness training programmes, remedial math and science programmes, career counselling programmes. They have provided significant resources, careful attention to the problems of women, and a commitment to improve the lot of women. They have helped some individuals succeed, and have turned out success stories to show for their efforts. But along with all the good that they do, they also embed the notion of women's inferiority within educational policy.

Rethinking the Deficit Model

Focussing on individual deficiencies may have some popular

appeal, and may even lead to some useful school programmemes, but it is not good enough, politically or analytically. A focus on what is wrong with girls (or women, or minorities or poor families) turns attention away from larger political structures. It is an approach that William Ryan has identified as "blaming the victim". [16]

Such an approach devalues the skills and attitudes of women, suggesting they are bad because they lead to low achievement. This not only avoids political criticism of the organization of the labour market, the school, and the state, but it also fails to account for women's experience of school.

To bring women up to the level of men is not what a socialist and feminist politics is about. We need to explore a more radical politics of opportunity.

There are three issues that are misrepresented by applying a deficit model to women's educational achievements. We need to think again about whether women achieve less than men, what differences in course enrolments mean, and how education is linked to the labour market.

1) Measuring Achievement

Looking for ways to explain and improve women's levels of achievement assumes that women do achieve less than men. But it is not at all clear that they do. Concern over women's lack of educational attainment obscures the fact that women perform as well as, if not better than, men in school. The educational attainment of men and women in Canada is virtually equal. Men in 1981 had, on the average, 11.9 years of schooling. Women, on the average, have 11.8 years of schooling. In 1971, men had 10.5 years and women had 10.6. Girls drop out of high school less often than boys.

As noted before, women's educational advantage through high school was even more pronounced in the past than it is today. In 1900 in B.C. women were 63% of all secondary students. Only in 1950 did the number of males aged 15-19 who were still in school catch up with the number of girls aged 15-19 who were in school.

More women than men have enrolled in community colleges. And women's proportion of the university enrolment has grown to over half. Between 1975 and 1986, female university enrolment increased by 35% compared to a 10.8% increase for males. In 1985-6, a total of 58% of undergraduates were women (61.7% of part-time students and 48.8% of full-time students). The percentage of bachelor and first professional degrees awarded to women has grown from 38% in 1970 to 44% in 1975 to 50% in 1980 and 53% in 1986.[17]

Although women are indeed at a disadvantage in the labour market, it is not clear that they are at a disadvantage in school. Girls are more likely to have a high school diploma, more likely to go on to a community college, and, as of a couple of years ago, more likely to attend university. While literacy, drop-out rates and low achievement levels remain a problem for the country as a whole, and while differences in achievement by social class persist, (and students from First Nations families leave school at an alarming rate), the girls seem to be coping as well, or as badly, as the boys. [18]

These figures tell the story using conventional measures of achievement. But the critique can be taken further. Whether women do or do not achieve as much as men depends on what counts as achievement. Feminists began to look at the definition of achievement and the scales that are used to evaluate performance. Debates about how poorly women perform in math and science depend partly on whether one looks at school grades, where girls do well, or at standardized test scores, where they do less well. Large scale testing agencies argue that standardized scores measure achievement more accurately because they exclude the personal assessments that teachers make and force all students to perform under similar, and very stressful, circumstances. But women argue that school grades are a more accurate measure because they include a more comprehensive assessment and allow achievement under diverse conditions to be taken into account.

The issue of scales and measuring levels of achievement is not a technical issue, but a political one. The question is what the school values and rewards.

One example of how the scales of measurement tend to favour men comes from the field of moral development. Theorists from Sigmund Freud to Lawrence Kohlberg had argued that here women perform less well than men. Women seemed to use forms of moral reasoning that are less "developed" than the forms of reasoning men use, and the forms of reasoning philosophers value, and schools teach.

But Carol Gilligan, a former student of Kohlberg, argued that the reason for women's apparent inferiority was based in the ways moral reasoning was assessed.[19] Kohlberg's famous six stages of moral reasoning were developed exclusively from studies of boys and men. Gilligan argued that the schemes do not reflect the ways women tackle moral dilemmas, and she undertook research to understand the way women think about moral action. Women are more likely to talk about responsibility and connection, she argues, when they are facing moral dilemmas. Men talk about autonomy and individual rights.

Rethinking scales of moral development led Gilligan into rethinking what counts as moral reasoning, and exploring the ways in which women reason differently from men. Who is more moral depends on what one thinks is adequate moral reasoning in the first place. Traditional scales have simply ignored women's ways of doing things, and have measured everyone on men's scales. What we need to do is rediscover the strength of women's ways of approaching problems, and to develop scales that value and reflect these.

Mary Belenky and her co-authors argue more broadly that women's "ways of knowing" are different from men's and devalued by the educational institutions and measures that men have devised.

Relatively little attention has been given to modes of learning, knowing and valuing that may be specific to, or at least common in, women. It is likely that the commonly accepted stereotype of women's thinking as emotional, intuitive and personalized has contributed to the devaluation of women's minds and contributions, particularly in Western technologically-oriented cultures, which value rationalism and objectivity.[20]

This kind of critique challenges the whole basis of what we do in schools, what we admire, and encourage and teach—in fact what we count as high achievement. It argues that the question of equal achievement is bound up with the most fundamental questions of value that feminists and educators ask.

2) Understanding Differential Course Enrolment

In the real world of education and of work, males and females are very often not engaged in the same kinds of activities and are therefore not evaluated on the same scales of achievement. Their work, their play, their schooling, each is frequently segregated. There are women's jobs and men's jobs; there are female courses and male courses.

With the segregation of male and female areas, the sexes do not compete directly against each other. Whatever women and girls do, however, tends to be devalued relative to whatever men and boys do.

This happens frequently in schools. The courses and programmemes dominated by women are treated differently from the courses and programmemes dominated by men. Women achieve in the humanities; men in science. Girls achieve in typing; boys in woodworking. The areas in which men study and work have higher prestige than the areas in which women study and work. Graduates from engineering earn more than graduates from nursing. Wage rates are higher for plumbers than for secretaries. It is clear that people with credentials in "male" areas get paid more, and exercise more power as adults. It is quite understandable, given these differences, that one aim of women activists has been to get more women into male areas of work.

This struggle by the women's movement—for equal access to high wages and positions of power—has been difficult and important. Young women seem to choose a remarkably few occupations at the moment, and broadening their vision of work is important. The crowding of women into a few (usually low paid) fields has prevented them from expressing the diversity of their interests, aptitudes and enthusiasms. And traditional women's work, already undervalued, is now being reorganized by technological change. This means that many traditional "women's" areas are disappearing.

Why do we value male areas more, and why do we pay men more for what they do? Largely because men have had the power to insist on the value of their work, and women have not been able to insist on the value of their's.[21] It is out of the realization that differences in value are rooted in differences in power that feminists have come to insist not just on equal pay for doing the same work as men, but on equal pay for work that may be different but is in fact of equal value.

Of course women should still be encouraged to take whatever jobs they find interesting and rewarding in the "male" domain. But the argument that women should go into male areas holds up what men have done as the model of excellence, and promotes the belief that women must be like men if they want money and power. It continues to devalue areas where women have excelled, and leaves unchallenged the fact that women who continue in these areas will get fewer rewards. It takes the structure of inequality for granted, while demanding that women not be relegated to the bottom rungs. And in doing this it abandons the struggle to revalue what women have always done.

One reason to insist on the full value of women's work is that it makes good strategic sense. If existing structures of power are left intact, some will move up, but the great majority will be left with little. Privileged and wealthy women will obtain the top positions at the expense of other women. In order to create a coalition where all groups can see their chances improve, we need to reduce inequality generally, and not be content with changing the sex of those at the top.

Another reason is plain justice. What women have traditionally done is important work that deserves to be treated with respect. Women who remain in traditional spheres are not "just" secretaries, nurses and housewives. Humanities should not have less status than the study of science and the study of technology. Concern and caring are not less important than achievement and competition. The social should not be devalued in relation to the technical. The question of equality becomes a question of the kind of world we want to live in.

Equality of opportunity, as we understand it today, does not mean merely enriching programmes to help girls catch up with boys. The aim and the result must be to increase the respect and the material rewards associated with what women do, as well as to encourage access for women to areas where men dominate. This means reexamining the entire curriculum, not just asking that women be added to parts of the curriculum from which they have been excluded.

3) Rethinking Connections to the Labour Market

A third problem with the deficit model is its simplistic assumptions about the links between school performance and economic success. In this model the reasons for economic disadvantage are located principally in schooling. Improvements in school performance are linked to improvements in job opportunities and income.

When researchers turn to school achievement to explain differences in the workplace, they are assuming that one of the important roles of education is to sort out students and allocate them to different positions in the labour market. Good students get A's, go on to university, and get professional jobs. Poor students get low marks, leave school early, and end up in poorly paid, less prestigious jobs. Or so the story goes. It is the meritocratic story on which schooling is based.

But this story misrepresents the nature of the labour market in some important ways. It ignores the fact that not everyone can get "good" jobs, even if everyone is very well-educated. It fails to examine critically the processes that are responsible for placing people in jobs. And it fails to explain why women get paid less than men when they are better educated.

Educational achievement does pay off at work. Those with more education are much less likely to be unemployed, and much more likely to earn high salaries and have high status jobs. In 1984, unemployment rates were 13.4% for those with less than 9 years of education, 13% for those with high school education, 8.3% for those with a post-secondary certificate or diploma, and

4.6% for those with a university degree.[22] A study of 1982 post-secondary graduates showed that their average earnings in 1984 went up with the level of their degrees. The average salary was $15,000 for trade/vocational graduates, $18,000 for college graduates, $23,000 for those with bachelor's degrees, $32,000 for those with master's degrees and $34,000 for those with doctorates.[23] Education does clearly make a difference for women as well as for men. Increased education is correlated with an increase in women's salaries, a decrease in their unemployment rates, and an increase in their level of participation in the labour market, just as it is for men.

But the crucial point here is that women get much less than men do for each extra year of education they obtain. The most dramatic evidence of this is salaries. While increased education increases women's salaries, the increase is much less for women than it is for men and the salary that each level of education buys is much lower, as is shown in this chart from *Women in the Labour Force*, a government publication put out by Labour Canada.

Average Income by Education & Sex, Canada: 1983 [24]

Years of education	Female	Male
0-8	$ 7,137	$15,923
High school	9,960	18,686
Post-secondary	13,703	24,321
University degree	20,107	33,841

The average woman with a university degree earns barely more than the average man with a high school diploma. Differences persist at every level of education.[25] Equal education, in short, does not eliminate the inequality of pay that men and women receive for their work.

Since women who participate in the labour force are more highly educated than those who do not, women in the labour force have on average slightly more education than men in the labour force. But women are not preferred for higher paying jobs.

Asking *why not* raises fundamental issues about the relationship between education and work, skill and income. "Human capital theory" posits that more educated workers are more valuable to the employer, and will be more productive, so they are paid more.[26] "Screening" theorists argue that education simply acts as a filter, and those who learn more quickly and efficiently are given credentials certifying their ability to learn. Employers will then prefer to hire them.[27] "Credentialling theory" argues that those who succeed in school have cultural attributes that are preferred by employers for high status jobs. They know how to act appropriately, and are preferred by employers because of that.[28]

Each of these models is sex-blind about schooling and work. They simply do not capture or explain women's disadvantage in turning education into income. In fact, employers do not rationally assess the productive capacity of workers and allocate them to slots that are appropriate for their qualifications. The facts show otherwise.

The labour market is not a competitive marketplace where everyone has equal power and competes with everyone else. It consists rather of segregated pools of labour, organized on the basis of gender and race, and it depends on a system of credentials and seniority which has been historically-structured by the power of workers and the interests of employers. Workers with less power to insist on their worth have been paid less.

The "segmented" nature of labour markets is critical.[29] There is no single labour market where every job applicant is evaluated against every other job applicant on his or her merits. The labour markets in which women predominate are different from the labour markets in which men predominate.

The evidence of this segmentation of the labour market by sex is clear. Women are clustered in non-professional clerical, sales and service occupations. In 1984, women had 32% of managerial jobs, 79% of clerical jobs, 56% of service jobs and 43% of sales jobs. If occupational categories are broken down further, the differences are even clearer. Women are 75% of elementary school teachers, 88% of nurses and related workers, 97% of secretaries, but represent 8% of sales supervisors, 5% of dentists and 12% of insurance salespeople.[30] Women do jobs that are different from and lower paying than those that men do.

Attention to the gender segmentation in labour markets reframes the questions about education and the economy, and leads to research on how women are channelled into specifically female areas, where the rewards that are available for achievement are lower than they are in male areas.

Differential enrolment patterns in school tie women closely to this sex-segregated labour market. It is clear that girls are still under-represented in physical science courses, in mathematics, computer science and industrial arts. They are over-represented in business courses, in home economics, in languages and in the humanities. By the time students move on to community colleges and universities, the differences become more pronounced and obvious. But the groundwork is laid in the public school system.

Women's work is characterized by the requirement for extensive educational preparation prior to job entry. Teachers, librarians, clerical workers, and nurses, for instance, train at their own expense, and are qualified by their specialized credentials. Their jobs offer few opportunities for promotion; they have a "flat" career structure. Men move more frequently into jobs where general credentials provide for entry, while on-the-job training and promotion provide for upward mobility.[31]

To understand the historical roots of gender-segregated workplaces, their persistence, and their characteristics, we need to look at the way employers make hiring decisions, at the impact of unions and their defense of apprenticeships and seniority, at the organization of job categories and at employers' assumptions about women's commitment to the labour force. It is here we see the impact of sex on labour market positions and rewards. This analysis does not focus on the individual characteristics of particular women, but on the social structures that systematically set women apart and below. It focusses attention, not on differences in the characteristics women bring to the labour market, but on the organization of the labour market and the training system itself. The practical interventions it suggests focus on employers, unions, personnel policies, hiring procedures, educational requirements and the provision of on-the-job training.

Beyond Deficit Thinking: Gender Equity and Institutional Responsibility

We have argued that it is necessary to look at institutions, not just at individuals, to see how the structure of these institutions shapes patterns of school achievement and their rewards in the labour market. The corollary is policy and political action directed at institutional and social change, instead of at individual counselling and remediation.

Social change in schools must focus on what is taught to students through example and through the formal curriculum. The curriculum is the result of state directives as well as the day-to-day decisions of teachers. The extensive research on the content of curriculum which will be discussed in the next chapter constitutes a massive indictment of the sexism of the educational system. This research reveals a "chilly climate for women"[32] in many classrooms. The goal of this research and the political practice based on it has been to produce an education where girls and boys are provided with equal opportunities to learn. This involves attitude change among teachers, but it also involves administrative restructuring, curriculum reform and widespread social change.

Educators need to be concerned with producing equal learning, and with achievements that are equally valuable for all children. This may mean treating them differently. Clearly, for example, exposing blind children to the same curriculum as seeing children does not give them an "equal opportunity". Rosalie Abella in her important *Royal Commission on Equal Employment Opportunity* argued that to treat everyone the same may be to offend the notion of equality. "...Ignoring differences and refusing to accommodate them is a denial of equal access and opportunity...it is not fair to use the differences between people as an excuse to exclude them arbitrarily from equal participation."[33]

Abella proposes an attack on "systemic" discrimination, arguing that institutions must adapt to women's needs and produce equal results for women, as well as for other disadvantaged groups. She proposes that all institutions should collect statistics on women's performance, so that problem areas can be seen and attacked. The institutions would then be held responsible for producing equity in whatever ways this could be accomplished.

In 1984, the New Brunswick Advisory Council on the Status of Women, for example, applied this concept of equality of results to education. They proposed analyzing the participation of males and females in every programmeme and, if they were not equal, attacking the problem in a myriad of ways —"for if equality of results is not occurring, then, quite simply, the system is failing."[34] Accountability rests with educators; they must find ways to educate everyone equally.

What does this mean for intervention strategies? No single prescription. Career days, new guidance materials and math anxiety workshops may have an effect on what young women can do. Making the curriculum more "girl-friendly", getting rid of sexual harassment, and reducing the streaming of students may all have a dramatic effect on opportunities for young women in some schools. Intervention strategies focussed on young women, and intervention strategies focussed on teaching and curriculum and parents may all be appropriate in some cases. The responsibility of educators is to monitor their effect, and to try alternative strategies until something works.

The relationship between individual action and social structure is complex, and is in fact one of the fundamental problems of social theory. To focus on individual actions, such as a girl's choice of career, or her ability to use tools, is also to focus in some ways on social structure. Her choices and abilities have been formed in social settings, and if these choices and abilities change, the social settings in which other young women choose and learn will be different. But to focus on individuals as if they acted with a completely free "choice" misrepresents the nature of schools, and blames individuals for making perfectly logical choices inside oppressive environments. Yet to focus on institutions as if they could completely shape the ideas and action of students isn't sensible either. It underrates the potential of people to confront and change institutions.

To understand the processes that maintain sex inequity in the school, we have to look at it both from the point of view of the young women who have to make choices, and from the point of view of the teachers and counsellors within the institution.

Some research on students' so-called "choices" of courses illustrates the problem.[35] The research revealed that girls actively chose traditional clerical courses, not because they loved them or felt particularly suited to them, but because, given the context of their lives, these courses seemed useful, or at least less of a waste of time than other courses. The students saw themselves making choices, often creative ones, designed to resolve the dilemmas that arose out of the structure of schooling, femininity and work. They said that clerical courses prepared them for available jobs in a way that no other courses in the high school did, that they were easy courses, that they wanted to avoid the sexual harassment they experienced in predominantly male courses, and they said they had to take into account the fact that they would be the ones to stay home with children and take care of the domestic labour, and that in planning their work lives they had to anticipate this gendered world.

These young women persist in traditional course and job choices for a variety of reasons that make sense to them, and to us as we listen. To change their "choices" we need to bring about a lot of changes in the way schools are organized, and in the way the workplace and the family are organized. It is not simply a matter of enlightening young women, but a matter of opening more options that seem attractive to them. Changing their patterns of school achievement and enrolment involves changing the world they experience, not simply changing their ideals, desires and personalities. Many young women would love, in an ideal world, to be doctors and lawyers, and they think they ought to have equal opportunities. But in dealing with the world that they know, they choose something else.

By focussing on why young women do not create more opportunities for themselves, we tend to blame the victim for the problem, to locate in girls themselves the reasons for the persistence of sexual inequality. While efforts to give girls information about the world are important, the assumption that girls make non-traditional choices because they are misinformed and unenlightened is a mistake, empirically and politically. Our concern should be to make non-traditional choices more attractive and possible, not to force them on our reluctant young.

To make these choices more attractive and possible means focussing on how changes in schooling and in the world outside the school could increase the opportunities girls and women have for an education. It is to the changes in schooling that we turn in the next chapter.

FOOTNOTES

1 A. Prentice and S. Houston. **Family, School and Society in 19th Century Canada.** Toronto: Oxford University Press, 1975. pp. 253-255.

2 M. Gillett. **We Walked Warily: A History of Women at McGill.** Montreal: Eden Publishers, 1981; A. Prentice et al. **Canadian Women: A History.** Toronto: Harcourt Brace and Jovanovich, 1988.

3 L. Marks and C. Gaffield. *Women at Queen's University, 1895-1905: A Little Sphere All Their Own.* **Ontario History** 78:4, pp. 331-46, 1986.

4 A. Prentice, et al, op. cit. p. 131.

5 A. Prentice et al. op. cit. p. 133.

6 J. Coleman. *The Concept of Equal Opportunity.* **Harvard Educational Review.** 38:7-22:1968.

7 *Report of the Royal Commission on the Status of Women in Canada.* Ottawa, 1970. P. 171.

[8] A. M. Henschel. **Sex Structure**. Toronto: Longman's 1973.

[9] For examples of this kind of research see D. Kauffman and B. Richardson. **Achievement and Women**. New York: Free Press, 1982; Porter, Porter and Blishen. **Stations and Callings: Making it Through the School System**. Toronto: Methuen, 1982; J. Gaskell. *The Sex Role Ideology and the Aspirations of High School Girls*. **Interchange** 8:3, 1977.

[10] M. Horner. *Femininity and Successful Achievement: A Basic Inconsistency*. Bardwick et al. (eds.) **Feminine Personality and Conflict**. Belmont, California: Brooks/Cole Purblishing, 1970.

[11] Horner, op. cit. p72.

[12] Labour Canada. *When I Grow Up: Career Expectations and Apsirations of Canadian Schoolchildren*. Ottawa: 1986, pp. 56-7.

[13] Labour Canada, op. cit. p. 56.

[14] R. Restak in **CSSE News**, 1977.

[15] *Women in Science: Intervention Techniques to Retain Women in Mathematics and Science Studies*. Office of Admission/Liaison. York University, 1988. P. 14.

[16] W. Ryan. **Blaming the Victim**. New York: Vintage Books, 1971.

[17] For statistics on gender difference in educational achievement, see Picot. *The Changing Educational Profile of Canadians, 1961-2000*. Statistics Canada, 1980; *Women in the Labour Force*. Statistics Canada, 1986:67-74 Cat. No. LO 16-1578/87B.

[18] R. S. Abella. *Report of the Commission on Equality in Employment*. Ottawa: Minister of Supply and Services, 1984.

[19] C. Gilligan. **In a Different Voice**. Boston: Harvard University Press, 1982.

[20] M.Belenky et al. **Women's Ways of Knowing**. New York: Basic Books, 1986, p. 6.

[21] M. E. Gold. **A Dialogue on Comparable Worth**. New York: Industrial and Labor Relations Press, Cornell University, 1983; D. Treiman and H. Hartman. **Women, Work and Wages: Equal Pay for Jobs of Equal Value**. Washington, D.C.: National Academy Press, 1981.

[22] Statistics Canada, 1986.

[23] Secretary of State. *The Class of '84: Summary Report on the Findings of the 1984 National Survey of Graduates of 1982*.

Ottawa:Minister of Supply and Services, 1986.

[24] Statistics Canada. *Women in the Labour Force, 1985-6*, p. 51.

[25] M.S.Devereau and E. Rechnitzer. **Higher Education—Hired? Sex Differences in Employment Characteristics of 1976 Post-Secondary Graduates.** Ottawa: Minister of Supply and Services, 1980.

[26] G.S. Becker. **Human Capital Theory.** New York: Columbia University Press.

[27] M. Spence. *Job Market Signalling.* **Quarterly Journal of Economics** 7, pp. 355-74, 1973.

[28] R. Spence. **The Credential Society.** New York: Academic Press, 1979.

[29] *Women in the Labour Force, 1985-86*, op. cit.

[30] M. Boyd. *Occupational Segregation: A Review.* Labour Canada. **Sexual Equality in the Workplace.** Ottawa: Ministry of Supply and Services, 1982.

[31] W. Wolf and R. Rosenfeld. *Sex Structure of Occupations and Job Mobility.* **Social Forces** 56, pp. 823-84, 1978; J. Madden. **The Economics of Sex Discrimination.** Lexington, Mass: Lexington Books, 1973.

[32] *Project on the Status and Education of Women*, 1982.

[33] Abella, op. cit.

[34] *New Brunswick Advisory Council on the Status of Women*, 1984, p. 8.

[35] J. Gaskell and A. McLaren. **Women and Education: A Canadian Perspective.** Calgary: Detselig, 1988.

Chapter 2

What is Worth Knowing?
Defining the Feminist Curriculum

The questions that we have to ask and to answer about that (academic) procession during this moment of transition are so important that they may well change the lives of all men and women
forever. For we have to ask ourselves, here and now, do we wish
to join that procession, or don't we? On what terms shall we join
that procession? Above all, where is it leading us, the procession
of educated men?...Let us never cease from thinking—what is
this "civilization" in which we find ourselves? What are these
ceremonies and why should we take part in them? What are these
professions and why should we make money out of them? Where
in short is it leading us, the procession of the sons of educated
men."[1]

Virginia Woolf poses these questions in *Three Guineas*. We
may also ask, do we want to join the academic procession? The
answer depends on what kind of education we are offered, or as
Adrienne Rich puts it, what kind of education we can claim. This
is at the heart of the feminist critique, and the feminist debate.

What kind of education is of most worth, what kind of education is of little worth, and what kind of education is positively destructive? What should the curriculum look like? Who should define it? Who needs what kind of knowledge and why? Feminists have had much to say in answer to these questions, and they are questions which are central to any theory and politics of education.

From an historical perspective, we see that the feminist critique and the feminist vision of the curriculum changed in response to changing social contexts. Already at the turn of the century, the Canadian women's movement was arguing for the inclusion of subjects of particular concern to women in the school curriculum. The Women's Christian Temperance Union argued for including temperance, the Imperial Order of the Daughers of the Empire argued for including citizenship, and the Women's Institutes argued for including all of the above, as well as home economics, or as it was then labelled, "domestic science".2

The case of domestic science is interesting, as it highlights some thorny issues that persist today in debates about women's knowledge and the curriculum. In the United States in 1842, Catherine Beecher published *A Treatise on Domestic Economy*, a text which applied moral philosophy, psychology physiology, hygiene, botany, physics, chemistry and architecture to the problems of managing a home and raising children. Her goal was to have women's domestic work raised in status and value by recognizing the complexity of its tasks and the scientific base that should inform them. The importance of this knowledge would be established by its presence in the school curriculum. But the existence of gender differences was not challenged. Women's sphere was domestic, and women were the nurturers, the preservers of family harmony and social welfare. The question of equality was tackled by giving equal importance to the knowledge necessary for these complex tasks.

Adelaide Hoodless was the best known Canadian proponent of domestic science in the schools. She believed that women belonged in the domestic sphere, and that the domestic sphere should have equal status with the public one. Women's work was separate from, but equal to, men's. The school curriculum should reflect both the equality and the separateness.

But when domestic science was widely introduced into the schools, the change was seen only partly as a victory for women. It was also quickly seen to provide a "ghetto" for women, a low status alternative to the academic mainstream, a way to keep women separate and unequal.

The feminist argument later moved to favour an integrated curriculum, where girls and boys learned the same things, thereby bringing an end to the segregation of industrial education (male) and home economics (female). It was convincingly argued that the entrenchment of "women's knowledge" in the curriculum reproduced traditional gender divisions.

Today, the question of women's knowledge and women's ways of knowing are back again on the agenda. Again feminists are arguing that the gendered division of labour has meant that women have distinctive knowledge and tasks, and that these have not been represented adequately in the curriculum. Again women are asking whether sex and gender differences make a substantial difference in the ways women learn, and whether these differences have been respected in the organization of the school.

The issues that arise historically in home economics are issues that need to be addressed systematically for the entire curriculum. How can we combine the rejection of traditional stereotypes, with a positive acknowledgement of the experiences of women? How can we both recognize the importance of gender in the production and incorporation of knowledge, and transcend the way gender has organized our lives and knowledge in a patriarchal society? The feminist critique has no single voice. By exploring some of the debates we can clarify what it means to argue for a curriculum that is equitable for both girls and boys, men and women.

Stereotyping in the Curriculum

In 1970 the Royal Commission on the Status of Women concluded, after examining textbooks used to teach reading, social studies, mathematics and guidance courses, that the problem with the school curriculum was that "a woman's creative and intellectual potential is either underplayed or ignored in the education of children from their earliest years. The sex roles described in these textbooks provide few challenging models for young girls, and they fail to create a sense of community between men and women as fellow human beings."[3]

Numerous studies in the 1970's further documented the findings of the Royal Commission and criticized the omission of women from curricular materials. Studies done by teachers' federations, community groups and academics emphasized the destructive impact of sex stereotyping in the curriculum.[4] These studies revealed that women and girls were under-represented in school books, and that when they were represented, they were stereotyped. Boys were also stereotyped, but in more powerful and active roles. Little girls in elementary texts played with dolls while their brothers played baseball; mothers wore aprons and baked cookies, while fathers drove off to work; adult women were princesses and witches, while men were doctors and farmers.

The research, in combination with political lobbying, had an effect on the schools. Under pressure from women's groups, publishers and ministries of education across the country appointed advisory groups to screen educational texts and media, issued non-sexist guidelines and developed and published alternative materials. What we see being used in the classrooms has become more diverse and less stereotyped .

This is not to suggest that the problem has disappeared. The old books continue to be used in schools because of the costs of replacing materials. The implementation of non-sexist guidelines is more difficult than their promulgation.[5] In 1988, the Federation of Women Teachers of Ontario published *The More Things Change.... the More They Stay the Same,* a study of elementary readers in use in Ontario. They showed that the stereotyping that had been documented 20 years ago was still prevalent in Ontario texts. [6]

The methodology and the assumptions underlying this study reveal the authors' implicit politics of the curriculum. The authors use worksheets to record the numbers of male and female, adult and child characters, and the type of stories involved (fiction, non fiction, myths/legends). They then indicate the number of pages given to each character, and rate each character on themes like self actualization, moral development, occupation, activities and emotions or descriptive words.

The conclusions support the title—little has changed since 1970. Occupations in these texts continue to reflect a sex-segregated labour market—women are witches and men are truck drivers; women more often care for others while men are less emotional; the man "plays golf" while the woman "is a true and loyal friend"; the man is "charged and sentenced for robbery"; while the woman "joins husband flying to Montreal"; and so on. The authors argue that this is a problem. Stereotyping continues even after two decades of an active women's movement.

We agree there should have been more change, but the lack of change is not evident just in texts: it is in the organization of Canadian society. Labour market statistics tell us that occupations continue to be stereotyped, and studies of the division of labour in the home tell us that women do more nurturing. These texts continue to reflect a fundamental reality—the sexual division of labour. The question is what relationship texts and the school curriculum should have to the world outside the schools. Should texts portray a world that is better than the real world?

The authors of the FWTAO study suggests they should. They argue that texts should portray an ideal and non-sexist world so that youngsters learn what is possible for them, and for the world at large. "Children must meet females and males in equal numbers who are intelligent, independent and competent"; males "should be shown receiving help, friendship and advice from females and as often as females receive these from males", "human failures should be portrayed as learning or growth experiences and not as events which stigmatize individuals for life" and so on.

One problem with these recommendations is that any portrayal of a traditional woman, or of a woman participating in traditional activities becomes a stereotype, and therefore is problematic. Secondly, the notion that all experiences are "positive growth experiences" would make it difficult to discuss the holocaust or slavery or racism. The world in children's books would be a good world. But it would not help children recognize and learn to deal with their own experiences.

We want children to see their experience reflected in their texts, not to create a new world of androgynous superpeople, and not to exclude material that shows women in traditional roles. Women do bake cookies and care for others. These activities must not be identified exclusively with women, of course, but the fact remains that women do them more often than men. A non-sexist curriculum should show mothers as secretaries as well as carpenters and girls playing with dolls as well as playing baseball.

Moreover, the world can be a nasty and unsafe place, with war and pain and racism and suffering. Materials showing racism in that connection are not out of place. We believe that children should be helped to see the world as it is, while being encouraged to develop a critical consciousness, a sense of active and cooperative participation that equips them to engage in the struggle for social change.

What is important is the ideology that underlies the images and the facts that are brought together in the curriculum. The underlying assumptions and story lines in the curriculum—what is being said about those images and characters—these should be the object of our critique. The number of male and female characters, the number of male and female doctors, the number of men and women baking cookies, can tell us something important. But only in context, only in light of the narrative, and its underlying message. The number of positive and negative evaluations of characters that are male and female can also be important, but how they are being judged, by whom and for what purposes, is the important question.

The fundamental issue is our conception of a non-sexist (or gender equitable, or feminist) curriculum and its relationship to a democratic and socialist curriculum. It involves more than avoiding stereotypes. It means incorporating knowledge that reflects the diverse experiences of women into what is deemed to be important school-based knowledge. It involves working from the experience of all children to introduce them to the varieties of experience that are possible, and how that variety can be understood. It involves changing our conceptions of many traditional disciplines and subject areas to make room for this knowledge. It means providing "really important knowledge" for women as well as for men, and it means bringing up gender issues in the classroom, for discussion and examination.

Reformulating the Problem: Giving a Voice to Women

Feminism has meant trying to give a voice to women, and allowing women to examine their own experiences, instead of always examining men's experiences. It has meant an effort to see the world from "the standpoint of women", in Dorothy Smith's phrase, and to make that part of the public discourse. While doing this we must keep in mind the diversity of women's experiences, and not allow white middle-class women's experience to stand for the experience of all women. There is no one place where women stand, and feminism means understanding the ways women have been silenced and women's experience has been misrepresented to themselves and to others.

Marge Piercy expresses the alienation and anger many women feel in relation to the world of intellectual, abstracted, male discourse in her poem "In the men's room(s)".

When I was young I believed in intellectual conversation:
I thought the patterns we wove on stale smoke
floated off to the heaven of ideas.
To be certified worthy of high masculine discourse
like a potato on a grater I would rub on contempt,
suck snubs, wade proudly through the brown stuff on the floor.
They were talking of integrity and existential ennui
while the women ran out for six-packs and had abortions
in the kitchen and fed the children and were auctioned off.
......

Now I get coarse when the abstract nouns start flashing.
I go out to the kitchen to talk cabbages and habits.
I try hard to watch what people do.
Yes, keep your eyes on the hands, let the voice go buzzing.
Economy is the bone, politics is the flesh,
watch who they beat and who they eat,
watch who they relieve themselves on,watch who they own.

The rest is decoration.[7]

The poem moves from the experience of trying to participate in male academic discourse, while always experiencing one's inadequacy as a woman, through to the rejection and distrust of that discourse. The woman in the poem concludes by distrusting abstraction, holding only to the immediacy of women's experience.

The response is a common one, but, we would argue, it is ultimately unhelpful. Our commitment is to reformulate academic discourse so that it does speak to women's experience, so that women can find a place for themselves in it. Piercy points to the two central problems. One is the lack of relation between theoretical, academic talk and the experience of women. The other is the exploitation of women that allows men the space and time to involve themselves in the abstracted talk that goes on in the academy.

Feminists must then ask what kind of curriculum can be important and relevent for women; what kind of a curriculum can integrate theory with the practices of women's lives, allowing students to assess critically the grounds of their exploitation and to work for change .

These concerns are not limited to women, of course. At a recent discussion of First Nations education, when students were complaining about the content of courses they were taking at the University of British Columbia, they used similar words, and focussed on the ways in which curriculum did not reflect or illuminate their experience as native people. "The concepts have been developed from the Western world....we need to start by describing our world....we haven't had a chance to reflect on our own experience and develop it...others are talking a different language", and so on. The problems, and the language used to express them, were uncannily similar to the arguments women have been making about the difficulty of using theories and language based in male experience, and the necessity of rethinking everything in order to accommodate their concerns.

And the argument has been made many times in relation to social class, as Ken Osborne documents in the first book of this series.[8] "There can be no doubt that existing curricula are biased, both in what they include and in what they omit; nor that for many working-class students they have little interest or appeal...It is clear also that schools have been intended to serve as instruments of the dominant ideology, playing their part in reproducing the social order and maintaining cultural hegemony."

The implications of these arguments are that the experiences of women (and of First Nations people, working-class people, visible minorities and other disadvantaged groups) must be incorporated into the curriculum. Children from all these groups must come to feel that the schools are for and about them, not just for and about privileged white males. The purpose of schooling must be to "empower" (to use an overworked word these days) them, to give them the ability to participate fully in struggles, large and small, to gain respect, dignity and power.

Making the curriculum more "girl-friendly" is one way of thinking about incorporating women's experiences into the school. This is articulated most often in connection with non-traditional courses, and it involves changes in curriculum content as well as in pedagogy. Science classrooms where teachers intervene to ensure equal participation, and where women scientists are discussed, make girls feel that science is for them. Science classes where the social issues associated with scientific discoveries are discussed are more popular with girls, who like to see the social significance and meaning of what they learn.[9] Girl-friendly schooling can also mean adding special classes in mathematics and science to give girls the extra experience with tools and mathematical problems which they need, and may allay their "math anxiety".

Adding women's experience to the curriculum can be done in a wide variety of ways across curriculum areas. In history texts incorporating women means adding discussions of women's suffrage, women's participation in the fur trade, and the changing organization of family life, as well as discussing why women were traditionally excluded from positions of power. In English classes it means examining novels and poems written by women, and seeking to understand why nineteenth century women writers used male names. In art classes it means rediscovering the work of women artists and asking why males produced "art" while women produced "crafts". In short, it means adding the study of women's experience to what has been a curriculum based on male experience. And it means understanding ways in which gender has shaped every discipline by excluding women's experience from that which schools have traditionally deemed worthy of study and analysis.

We must also bear in mind the diversity of the female experience, and not fall into the trap of reifying "the" female experience, which will turn out to be the experience of more privileged women. Curriculum change must involve a dynamic process which enables women to speak from all the places they occupy in the world.

To include women's experience means diversifying the curriculum so that native women, children from single parent homes, businesswomen and Chinese-Canadian women see what they are taught as having some relevance for their lives, so that the enormous variety of women's experience in Canada is represented in instructional settings.[10] It means adding the study of Audre Lorde's poems to the curriculum, alongside Virginia Woolf's novels. It means adding the study of women's work in First Nations families in Labrador as well as adding the study of pioneer women in Nova Scotia.

The so-called "integration" debate around women's studies raises the question of whether adding women's concerns and women's experiences to the curriculum is a process of addition or a process of transformation.[11] Those who want to keep women's studies as a separate course, department or field argue that cooperative, contextual and interdisciplinary feminist scholarship can only arise and be carried forward among a group of similarly committed educators and students. They argue that the development of women's scholarship depends on a like-minded community of women who are not preoccupied with fighting against male structures. They argue that the knowledge is of most value to women, and that women are the ones who must struggle for change, since they are the ones who are the most open to exploring its meaning.

The advocates of integration, on the other hand, argue that feminist scholarship must develop alongside, be incorporated into and ultimately transform the mainstream disciplines, and the curriculum which all students learn. They argue that women's studies becomes a ghetto that allows most students to continue in "men's studies".

We are clearly on the side of those who argue that the ultimate goal is not to continue with two versions of knowledge, the male version and the female version, but to develop a new synthesis that is richer for paying attention to both male and female perspectives. Transforming the entire curriculum, and the entire body of what we count as knowledge must be our ultimate objective. Women's studies programmes are essential in this struggle, but they are not all that is needed.

To add women's experience to the curriculum means fundamental change. It means re-examining the rules that are used for inclusion in the first place and changing the way the entire subject is conceptualized. If the people mentioned in history texts are those who have played an important role in governing the country, clearly women cannot be equally represented. The process of adding women involves changing ideas about what students should learn in history classes and why they should study history in the first place. It means learning about the ways ordinary people lived their lives so children can understand the history of people like themselves. It means including more social history, more studies of how families were organized and work was distributed in other historical periods. It means understanding the ways sex and gender have shaped the organization of Canadian society.

The omission of women is not just a question of oversight. Our very conception of education, of what is worth knowing, and of the disciplines which are studied is challenged by the process of including women. Adding the experiences of women means a reworking of knowledge from its very roots. "Malestream" thought, as Mary O'Brien has dubbed traditional scholarship,[12] is revealed as partial, based in male experience, and therefore inadequate. Seemingly objective and value-free inquiry is revealed to be based on male assumptions.

One of the most influential Canadian documents to address the way feminism must transform all knowledge was published in 1985 by the Social Sciences and Humanities Research Council. Margrit Eichler and Jeanne Lapointe point out that scholarship that does not take adequate account of women is simply bad scholarship.

As long as women were de facto excluded from intellectual work and higher education, sex-related bias in research was not widely recognized as a problem for the social sciences and humanities. Culture and our way of thinking were shaped by a male perspective which applied even when the life, identity and thought of women were considered. There was little or no awareness that such an androcentric perspective generates serious intellectual problems. Central concepts were seldom examined with respect to their applicability to both sexes, and sexist language was usually uncritically accepted, in spite of its inexactness. [13]

The pamphlet goes on to give specific examples of how male bias operates and what can be done about it. Eichler and Lapointe discuss how research has mistakenly transformed statistical differences into innate differences (as in psychological scales of masculinity and femininity), over-generalized concepts that apply to males ("universal" suffrage was granted before women got the vote) and failed to consider the way assumptions about sex and gender affect data gathering ("Do you think women doctors are as good as men doctors?" does not allow the response that women are better doctors).

Awareness of these biases in traditional scholarship has informed the development of a feminist scholarship that has been having an impact on academic work in every discipline and field of study. Although the progress remains slow and far from even, the incorporation of this work into the school curriculum will transform it into a non-sexist body of knowledge.

This wide-ranging critique makes the process of putting women back into the curriculum a difficult, indeed revolutionary task. It is relatively straightforward (though we would not want to underplay the difficulty of some of these struggles) to put the suffragists and the First Nations women who organized the fur trade back into the history books, to add a few novels written by women into the literature curriculum, and to add some women artists to the arts syllabus. It is quite another thing to change the way we approach historical, literary and artistic study, and the criteria we use to assess its significance and value. It is nothing less than this that a socialist feminist politics demands.

The Educated Person

The values and politics inherent in any curriculum permeate the organization of classrooms and schools and the interactions between students and teachers, as well as the content of texts. Questions of curriculum content and pedagogy cannot be neatly separated. The question of how well the existing curriculum serves women includes questions about what is taught and how it is taught.

Adrienne Rich states the concerns and issues of the feminist classroom in her essay, *Taking Women Students Seriously*. She says,

> Listen to the voices of the women and voices of the men; observe the space men allow themselves, physically and verbally, the male assumption that people will listen, even when the majority of the group is female. Look at the faces of the silent and of those who speak. Listen to a woman groping for language in which to express what is on her mind, sensing that the terms

of academic discourse are not her language, trying to cut down her thought to the dimensions of a discourse not intended for her..."[14]

Social science has approached the problems with less nuance, but with some clear findings. There were some early and striking studies on classroom interaction that showed teachers paying much more attention to boys in class, and being quite unaware of this fact. Boys tended to be evaluated by teachers as more intelligent and inquiring, but less well-behaved. Girls were evaluated as more docile, more hardworking, more likely to get the right answer, but less intelligent. Girls were being penalized for doing what the teacher asked, both by getting less attention, and by being thought of as less capable in the long run.

Studies also documented a wide variety of ways in which girls and boys were treated, and how they acted, in clearly stereotyped ways in the classroom. Boys fetched the projectors, and girls cleaned the brushes. Girls did projects on seeds, and boys did projects on electric motors. Girls played in the doll corner while boys played in the big block corner. In science classes, boys "hogged" the equipment, while girls hung back, feeling incompetent. In computer classes, boys excluded girls from the informal groups which gathered around the terminals. Clearly issues of sex equity needed to be attacked in classroom behavior, not just in texts.

Much of this analysis tended to blame the teacher for the problem. Teachers held traditional stereotypes. Teachers needed workshops on gender equity in the classroom. And many teachers did need to re-examine their position on sex and gender issues, in their own lives as well as in relation to their students. But teachers were only part of the problem. Teachers respond to the already gendered behaviors of their students, and teachers work in schools which in a variety of ways are imbued with sexist assumptions.

The question of institutional, "systemic" sexism must be tackled by teachers and parents collectively. In focussing on the teacher, it is important not to forget the context in which s/he works. Policies calling for gender-inclusive language in school communication, affirmative action guidelines for hiring and promotion, commitment to school-based day care and respect for the work of mothering all express the school's interest in gender equity in ways that go beyond an individual teacher's action.

The interactions between student and teacher raise critical questions in relation to the teacher's responsibility in social matters. Some would argue that in democratic classrooms, teachers must respect the values of their students and the surrounding community, even if these values include restrictions on women. This is not a position we find politically responsible. Educators must value the development and growth of all students equally.

But the question of how to intervene effectively to open up possibilities to female students who want, for example, to continue to play only in the doll corner, or who do not want to speak up in class and argue with the boys, can be more complicated. And the question of how to end intimidation by the boys, how to get them to see sexual harassment for the problem it is, and how to encourage them to express their nurturant and expressive selves, can be even more difficult. A skilled teacher must work with patience, empathy and a firm commitment to equity, to create a classroom that works for both boys and girls.

A feminist approach to pedagogy is as complex as a feminist approach to content. We have argued that ridding the schools of stereotyping is a partial approach, based in liberal assumptions, not questioning adequately the organization of schooling. In thinking about feminist pedagogy, we need to examine the underlying assumptions about education and its purposes, to see how these have been based in male experience, and to reframe them in ways that take the experiences of women seriously.

Jane Roland Martin has argued that both the content and the structure of schooling have been designed to prepare young people for a male world. The school has been justified as preparation for the public, productive sphere, for work and for citizenship. In the public sphere, men have played dominant roles, and women have been excluded, by custom, tradition, or law. "The idea of the humanities was tied to civic life and leadership in the public arena...The humanities have been tied to an ideal of human commonality, a unity based on the ideal of the cultivated, educated gentleman." [15]

Schooling has ignored the private sphere. Learning for family life, for the reproductive processes of the society have been relegated to the family. As a result, Martin argues, the ideal of the educated person has been based in the male stereotype—objective, analytic, rational, interested in ideas and things, but not nurturing, empathic, intuitive or supportive. Education has emphasized the development and application of reason and objective judgment; it has separated the mind from the body, thought from action and reason from emotion. [16]

But even Jean-Jacques Rousseau, who outlined such a curriculum for his hero Emile, realized it was not adequate for a society. Rousseau assigned to Sophie, Emile's sister, the womanly arts of caring, bringing up children, and soothing the fevered brow of the public man. To educate the whole person, and to ensure the survival of our society, Martin argues, we must not ignore those tasks and qualities that have been assigned to women and to the private sphere; rather, we must integrate them into the mainstream, into the public school system. We must build nurturing capacities and an ethics of care into the curriculum for all our students, and not depend on women to learn it privately, and do it for us all.

Martin does not think, as women reformers did at the turn of the century, that this means incorporating home economics into the curriculum, even for male as well as female students. As Martin emphasizes,

> If education links nurturing capacities and the 3Cs (of caring, concern, and connection) only to subjects such as home economics that arise out of the reproductive processes, we will lose sight of the general moral, social and political significance of these traits. So long as rationality and autonomous judgment are linked exclusively with the productive processes of society, the reproductive ones will continue to be devalued...When the productive/reproductive dichotomy and its accompanying hierarchy of values is rejected, teaching methods, learning activities, classroom atmospheres, teacher-pupil relationships, school structures, attitudes towards education may all be affected. [17]

She further maintains that "not only are the goals of schooling primarily male and public, but the process by which knowledge is transferred in schools is based on male development."[18] The notion that male development and female development are fundamentally different is in some ways a dangerous one. Research on sex differences in learning and thinking is often based on the premise of women's inferiority, and is designed to explain it. It has been an attempt to explain why girls don't achieve as well as boys, and to document their deficits in school, as was pointed out in the previous chapter. Early feminists were very suspicious of an emphasis on difference, and wanted instead to emphasize the ways women were like men, and should therefore be treated like men, rather than being excluded and stereotyped.

However, a burgeoning feminist literature is now exploring the fact that sex and gender do make a difference in the ways we learn and reason. This is not primarily because of biological differences, although there are some provocative arguments about the effect of conceiving and giving birth, and about the effects of hormones and reproductive cycles. It is rather because gender makes a difference to how people live, what toys they play with as children, who their friends are, how much power they are able to exercise in the world, and how others talk to them. It is then not surprising that researchers are able to document differences between men and women in the ways they learn best. And the question of which ways are best, and which ones should be rewarded and taught in schools must be openly examined and explored.

What is good for males is not necessarily good for females in schooling. If female students are learning in institutions which are based on male models of development, which value male skills and ways of reasoning, and which pay more attention to male learning, they are not getting an equal education.

Notions of good moral behaviour are central to any school organization. In the previous chapter we discussed how ways of measuring good moral reasoning need to take gender into account. Women have been described as holding more often to an ethic of care, basing morality in a sense of connectedness and responsibility, rather than in a version of universal rules and individual rights. Most schools are organized around an ethic of rights, rather than an ethic of caring. An ethics of rights emphasizes individual autonomy, but as Gilligan says, "it may appear frightening to women in its potential justification of indifference and unconcern. At the same time...from a male perspective, a morality of responsibility appears inconclusive and diffuse given its insistent contextual relativism." [19]

A recent book, **Women's Ways of Knowing**,[20] explores differences between the ways men and women learn to understand their relationship to knowledge. The authors argue that women come to understand knowledge as constructed, not given, as connected to, not separated from experience. The authors call for "connected teaching", arguing that women are more likely to learn in ways that explore and relate their experience to the curriculum. They call for problem posing, instead of lecturing, for the teacher as "midwife", instead of imparter of knowledge, for a "yoghurt" class, which provides a culture for growth, as opposed to a "movie" class , where the students are spectators.

As Adrienne Rich puts it, we must teach our students to think like women, not to try to think like men:

> Men in general think badly: in disjuncture from their personal lives, claiming objectivity where the most irrational passions seethe, losing, as Virginia Woolf observed, their senses in the pursuit of professionalism. It is not easy to think like a woman in a man's world, in the world of the professions; yet the capacity to do that is a strength which we can try to help our students develop. [21]

It is radical to insist that schooling recognize the importance of nurturing as well as independence, community as well as individualism, caring as well as responsibility. While it may be possible to formulate plans to stop discrimination against female students and encourage interaction between teachers and female students, it is much more difficult to incorporate a feminist pedagogy that challenges bureaucracy, hierarchy and competition in educational institutions, and a curriculum that joins emotion to reason, and personal experience to knowledge.

These calls for a pedagogical shift have a long and distinguished history. Educators from John Dewey to Paolo Friere to Sylvia Ashton-Warner have argued for a similar shift, and called for an education that will work from the experience of all learners to a pedagogy that is more effective and a society that is more democratic. The feminist critique, in raising questions about who schooling should be for, and how to change it, shares and adds to a long democratic and socialist tradition of educators calling for change.

The Possibilities of Change

Studies of the problems of education frequently make the problems so clear and so overwhelming that they leave little room for hope. A more complete political analysis does not end in despair: it inspires work for change, provides some general vision of alternatives, and leaves people with the energy and enthusiasm to try to bring about changes in their own way.

The feminist movement has brought about change in education, and these changes are ones we should celebrate as well as learn from. In this section we will report some of the changes that have taken place in the Toronto Board of Education. Toronto is not representative of Canadian school districts by any means. It has had a staff person specifically responsible for Women's Studies since 1975. Only seven Boards of Education in Ontario and a few in other Canadian jurisdictions have created similar staff positions. The changes that have taken place in Toronto are changes worth reflecting upon and learning from.

An informal group of Toronto teachers met in 1988 to assess the effects of women's studies and affirmative action efforts in their schools. Members of the group were unanimous in their belief that sex role stereotyping had diminished, that consciousness about the role and contributions of women had been raised, and that numerous sexist practices had been substantially dismantled. Elementary school teachers reported that girls' lines and boys' lines were a thing of the past, that the classroom housekeeping area was now sex-integrated, that *The Paper Bag Princess* had become a modern classic, and that while school libraries had not ditched most sexist children's books, at least they had added numerous titles which portrayed girls and women in a positive light.

Although men still outnumber women in positions of responsibility in elementary as well as secondary schools, the Toronto Board of Education has incorporated affirmative action goals and timetables into its employment policies for teachers to increase the number of women in areas in which they were under-represented. Females in positions of responsibility are clearly more visible and more numerous in this jurisdiction. Few, if any, students now go through public school without seeing and being influenced by women administrators.

As computers are introduced across the curriculum they are accompanied by computer equity guidelines with strategies for encouraging all students to use computers and with specific suggestions for teachers to discourage male dominance around the new technology. Similarly, male dominance in the area of athletics has been recognized and a recent report on equal opportunity in school athletics attempts to move toward equality in what has traditionally been a most unequal arena. What are some of the other areas of change?

Language

Language reflects consciousness. Language describes the way in which we see the world. The conscious use of non-sexist language in both speech and print describes the world in gender-inclusive terms and helps to build a less sexist future.

Heated discussions about changing sexist language habits have raged in many staff rooms. Gradually the shrill voices of opponents to the use of non-sexist language as well as the lethargy of those for whom changing language appeared too large an ordeal, are being challenged by those who see language as an issue of power and who see inclusive language as a positive step toward equity. Many boards, including the Toronto Board of Education, have drafted and are implementing inclusive language policies.

School Action Plans

Reducing sexism in institutions as large and varied as school systems is a formidable task. The Toronto Board of Education requires each elementary and secondary school to appoint a women's studies representative (in large schools this may be a committee) whose task is to design, implement and evaluate a single manageable goal to reduce sexism in each school year. The plan must be discussed and approved by staff members and sometimes includes student and parent voices. A coordinator of women's studies helps schools consider appropriate goals, offers information on ideas which have proven successful in other jurisdictions, and provides some funding to implement plans.

The process of having each school reconsider its women's studies goal(s) on an annual basis gives the message that sexism is deep-rooted and will not be eliminated overnight. At the same time it allows schools to see that their work on the issue can make a difference. At the Toronto gathering in 1988, teachers whose schools had designed and implemented plans for ten years unanimously indicated that they felt their school plans had helped raise consciousness and reverse overt sexist practices. These teachers are now prepared to work on identifying and dealing with covert sexist practices and habits.

When each school is allowed to identify its own goal(s) rather than having to respond to a centrally-dictated, system-wide priorities, the uniqueness of each school community is recognized and local initiatives can be developed. In 1988, one school took advantage of the Olympics and focussed its plan on equal opportunity in sports. Students researched and produced a school-wide visual display on women's contributions and achievements in sports through the 20th century. The same school is also in the process of analyzing budgets for athletic programs and making recommendations to assure that funding of men's and women's physical and health education programmes is equalized.

Another school identified math anxiety among girls as its key area of concern. The school implemented a family math programme in which English and non-English speaking parents spent five evenings in the school library playing math-based games and doing activities with their children. More games were distributed to parents for the summer so that male and female children would continue to experience parental involvement in mathematics-based activities.

A third school decided its key goal was to encourage girls in the sciences. This school organized a school-based Mini-Science Fair and all staff encouraged female students to participate in preparing projects for the fair.

A fourth school designed a 3-week block in which the role and contribution of women in every discipline was emphasized. The art course studied women's contribution to ceramics and sculpture. The science programme focused on ecology and emphasized women's contribution to the environmental protection movement. English students read women authors and history students looked at the role of women in the anti-apartheid struggle in South Africa. The block ended with a full-day school celebration of "Women in Action" which featured participatory discussions, a panel discussion on Prostitution and Sex Trade Workers, and entertainment.

While school-based plans do allow each school to consider its own needs, some larger jurisdictions are simultaneously designing system-wide projects which are not financially feasible for a single school.

A popular initiative has been launched in Toronto and other Ontario boards of education with the *Expanding Your Horizons* conferences for young women students. The goal of these conferences is to encourage young women to consider mathematics, science and computer education for their future career choices. With hands-on activities and female role models who use those disciplines in their work, these special days encourage young women to pause and explore options beyond stereotyped career choices for women and to consider the kind of preparation students will need to enter these fields. Borrowing a model developed in California, boards of education have run these special days for students from Grades 7-12/13. The Toronto Board of Education has also designed a workshop for parents which not only gives parents information about math/science education and their daughters' career choices, but also allows parents to come to terms with their own anxieties and uncertainties about the world of work awaiting their daughters.

Another system-wide initiative which can be adopted by single schools involves the *Job Site Visits* project sponsored by the Toronto Board of Education. In this programme teachers and students visit work sites in which career people (usually women) are working in mathematics or science-related careers. Rather than have the community visit the school (as in *Expanding Your Horizons*) in *Job Sites* the school visits the community and students get to see various work processes first hand, and to meet positive female role models in non-traditional career settings.

Learning Materials

The Toronto Board of Education now screens every curriculum document for sexist (as well as racist and class-biased) language and images. An Advisory Council on Bias in the Curriculum which includes teachers, principals, vice-principals, as well as parent representatives from ethnic liaison groups, performs an important monitoring function. Many suggestions from this committee have been incorporated in completed documents. At the recommendation of the committee, all curriculum writers will soon be given in-service training on race, sex and class bias before writing projects begin.

The Ontario Ministry of Education has developed criteria for defining bias in curriculum; all documents submitted for inclusion on Circular 14, an annual publication of approved texts for use in Ontario schools, are now sent to outside evaluators who specifically analyze texts for sex role stereotyping as well as ethnocultural and racial bias. In 1984, 29 of 179 submissions for inclusion on the list were rejected because of perceived bias and/or stereotyping.

Because of budget constraints, the shelf life of many text books is 15 to 20 years. Even some of the new materials are disappointing in their portrayal of women. Nevertheless, conscious and energetic educators have much better materials to use than were available in 1970. The Toronto Board of Education has opened a Women's and Labour Studies Resource Room which includes thousands of books, vertical files, photographs, audio-tapes, posters, slides and other learning materials for teacher and student use. While Canadian materials are not as abundant as American sources (the U.S. based National Women's History Project publishes a 36-page catalogue of outstanding classroom materials), the long drought of materials portraying women's experience in all facets of life is mercifully coming to an end.

In the meantime, it is the responsibility of boards of education to train teachers to deal critically with stereotyped materials. One lesson plan designed by the California-based National Women's History Project and adapted from Stereotypes, Distortions and Omissions in U.S. Texts by the Council on Interracial Books for Children, could be used by Canadian teachers. The activity involves identifying sexist, racist, or class-biased passages from their own textbooks. Based on additional material and their own research, students are asked to rewrite these offensive and distorted passages.

What About the Boys?

Education programmes are being developed to increase awareness of a broad range of work options based on skill and interest rather than on stereotyped notions of what is appropriate for each sex. While many of these programmes place their emphasis on getting girls and young women to consider non-traditional occupations, few are directed to young men who need encouragement to explore the possibility of entering arts-based careers or nurturing occupations. While the economic motivation for women to move into non-traditional careers far exceed the personal reasons for males to consider what have been "female careers", our eventual goal must be to eliminate gender as a factor in all people's career selection.

A unique programme run in the Toronto area is *Boys for Babies*. This brief hands-on course is designed for pre-adolescent males (grades 5-6), and attempts to break down male stereotypes about sex-appropriate behaviour and activities. Boys are withdrawn from their regular school programme and are given an opportunity to care for, learn about, and bond with infants who are brought in from the community. At the beginning most boys express the stereotyped belief that infant care is "women's work". Over the course of a month, however, the boys begin to change their own notions about whether care-giving should be restricted to one sex. In this environment the nurturing, caring, and sensitive behaviour of the boys is encouraged. At the end of four two-hour sessions most young men have had a positive experience and have reflected on the ways in which care-giving can be satisfying and positive.

In a draft manual entitled *Snakes and Snails*, the Toronto Board of Education suggests dozens of activities for students in grades 4-8 which focus on male sex role stereotyping. The Introduction of *Snakes and Snails* makes the point that "young boys need permission and encouragement to learn about nurturing. Girls also need to see models of male nurturers." The manual includes interviews with males doing non-traditional work, suggests community service experiences that will give students practice in being care-givers, and includes improvisations, tableaux, and role plays which encourage discussion about male and female sex role stereotyping. Practical work in classrooms with *Snakes and Snails* not only encourages males to consider non-traditional work and to redefine maleness, but also encourages boys to accept a broader range of options for their female peers. This is important because research has shown that male peer expectations are an important influence on girls' academic course choices and career selections.

Gender Communications

Researchers Myra and David Sadker have found that in the United States, "Male students receive more attention from teachers and are given more time to talk in the classroom."[22] Male students are generally involved in more interactions than female students. The Sadkers found that males receive more positive comments, more criticism, and more remediation.

Males tend to clog the air waves. A Toronto teacher, disturbed by the domination of male students in his secondary school classroom, asked students to use a stop watch to measure how much males and females were speaking in the class. Students themselves were shocked by the results. Males were speaking 75-80% of the time.

Most educators are generally unaware of gender communications bias. They believe that they treat males and females equally but are unaware of gender difference in the way they question male and female students, in the waiting time allowed for male or female students to answer questions, in the patterns of interruption, and in the kind of feedback given to male or female students. According to the Sadkers, brief but focussed training is effective in changing teacher behaviour.

Representing the Diversity of Women's Experiences

In our efforts to create more choices for women, we must not invalidate women who make traditional choices. In preparing a curriculum guide for Grade 4 students in Toronto called *Working in the City: Kids Talk to Workers About What They Do,* educators debated whether to include a portrayal of women whose work was secretarial along with a portrayal of a female electrician. Some educators argued that children see enough women in traditional roles in real life and that progressive curriculum should only portray women in non-stereotyped roles. Others argued that in our frenzy to create new images we must not invalidate the role and contribution of those who have done, now do, and will in the future do traditional female work. We must not insult these women, and we should not be in the business of judging which occupational categories are "superior" for our daughters and female students. In the end, both portrayals were included in the text.

Empowering Young Women

Mary Kay Thompson Tetreault has stated "There is little in the schools which educates female students to think about their rights and responsibilities in shaping their own lives."[23] She implores teachers "to help girls of various classes and races think about their futures."

A systematic effort is needed to develop curriculum that includes necessary information about the work force, the changing family, the legal system, services available in the community, and ways to make responsible changes in one's personal life and in the work place. Schools can also help empower female students through cooperative learning in classrooms, and through full participation in student government, in school athletics, in science fairs and in cultural events. Schools can recognize, acknowledge and use the cooperative, nurturing and organizational skills young women bring to schools, and they can teach young women leadership skills such as how to chair meetings and how to facilitate discussions. In Toronto, the *Expanding Your Horizons* Conference uses trained female senior high school students to facilitate discussions among grade 7 and 8 students.

Toronto has also run a special conference called *Life After High School* to give graduating students information about women's issues they are likely to encounter at home, in the work place and in the community.

Staffing and Funding

The creation of equal opportunity for female students in schools has a price tag. More and better materials have to be developed and purchased; staff training and retraining are necessary; research needs to be done on girl-friendly curricula; positive workshop models must be developed for parents and teachers so that both school and home can give students a consistent message about the goal of equality for women in society; leadership programmes for female students and staff as well as curriculum that supports nurturing behaviour in males and male acceptance of a wide range of opportunities for girls need to be developed, tested and implemented.

Even "progressive" boards of education hire only one person in a large school system to create women's studies programmes and affirmative action programmes; they allocate a pitiful budget, and consider the job done. Yet even inexpensive and simple things can make a big difference in the life of an individual learner.

Eve was a *straight-A* student in a Toronto alternative high school. University-bound, she suffered from neither math nor science anxiety. The school she attended made a conscious and continuing attempt to create a non-sexist environment and to give females equal voice, recognition and participation in every aspect of school life.

At Eve's school the community had decided to integrate the past and present contribution and participation of women into every discipline. The mathematics teacher was perplexed. Was not his discipline neutral? After discussion with other staff the mathematics teacher located and hung on his bulletin board a poster series of notable women in mathematics. He did not say a single word to his classes—he merely changed the visual environment of his classroom. After one period in this changed classroom, Eve was elated.

"I always knew I could do mathematics," Eve commented, "but I never thought of it as a field in which women had made a contribution. Those posters make me feel good."

Changing sexist schools into less sexist institutions is not, of course, just a matter of hanging up mass produced sets of posters. We have learned much about the layers of personal and institutional sexism standing in the way of equity. It will take many large and small efforts to forge change.

When Alice Baumgartner and colleagues at the Institute for Equality of Education and the University of Colorado surveyed 2000 children asking the question: "If you woke up tomorrow and discovered that you were a (boy/girl) how would your life be different?" she found that male and female students were almost unanimous in feeling that boys are better off than girls.[23] If schools are successful in reducing the level of sexism, and if Alice Baumgartner's research were repeated in the year 2000, perhaps we will find different results. In the next millennium we can strive for a population of females who do not feel that they will lose opportunities because of their sex and a population of males who will have learned to appreciate and acknowledge the contribution of females.

Addressing the content of the curriculum—what we teach our children about the world in which they live—is central to the agenda of feminism. We must ensure that what is taught and learned in schools does not degrade women, does not misrepresent our experience, or interpret it through the categories of malestream scholarship.

We must keep in mind that the demand is a radical one that involves restructuring our conceptions of worthwhile knowledge for all students.

FOOTNOTES

[1] Virginia Woolf. **Three Guineas**. New York: Harcourt, Brace, 1938., pp. 62-3, quoted in Adrienne Rich *Toward a Woman-Centred University,* in **On Lies, Secrets and Silence**. New York: W.W. Norton, 1979.

[2] N. Sheehan. National *Issues and Curricula Issues: Women and Eudcational Reform: 1900-1930* in Gaskell and McLaren, **Women and Education: A Canadian Perspective**. Calgary: Detselig, 1987.

[3] Royal Commission on the Status of Women, Ottawa, 1970.

[4] S. Pyke, *Children's Literature: Conceptions of Sex Roles* in E. Zureik and R. Pike, **Socialization and Values in Canadian Society**. Toronto: McClelland and Stewart, 1975; J. Gaskell, *Stereotyping and Discrimination in the Curriculum* in J.D. Wilson and H. Stevenson, **Precepts, Policy and Process: Perspectives on Contemporary Education**. Calgary: Detselig, 1977; L. Fisher and J.A. Cheyne, *Sex Roles: Biological and Cultural Interactions as Found in Social Science Research and Ontario Educational Media,* Toronto: Ontario Ministry of Education, 1977; Batcher et al., *And Then There Were None...*A Report commissioned by the Status of Women Committee, Federation of Women Teachers of Ontario, Toronto, 1975; *Women in Teaching Text Book Study,* British Columbia Teachers Federation, Vancouver, 1975; C. Pascoe, *Sex Stereotyping Study,* Halifax: mimeo, 1975; L. Cullin, *A Study into Sex Stereotyping in Alberta Elementary Textbooks.*Edmonton: mimeo 1972.

[5] P. Galloway, *What's Wrong With High School English? It's Sexist... unCanadian...outdated.* Toronto: OISE Presss, 1980. National Film Board, Report of the National Film Board/Education Forum on Women's Studies in Secondary School. Ottawa, 1986.

[6] FWTAO. *The More Things Change...The More they Stay the Same.* Toronto:1988.

[7] *In the men's room(s).* **To Be of Use Poems** by Marge Piercy. Garden City, NY: Doubleday and Co., 1973 ,p. 8.

[8] Ken Osborne. **Educating Citizens: A Democratic Socialist Agenda for Canadian Education**. Toronto: Our Schools/ Our Selves, 1988.

9 *See Who Turns the Wheel,* op. cit.; J. Whyte. **Girls into Science and Technology,** London: Routledge and Kegan Paul, 1986; and B. Collis. *Adolescent Females and Computers: Real and Perceived Barriers* in Gaskell and McLaren, **Women and Education.**

10 See, for example, *All in a Day's Work,* and *ESL Kit on the Value of Housework* by the Committee to Advance the Status of Housework, Toronto, 1981; *A Shared Experience: Bridging Cultures: Resources for Cross-cultural Training,* Cross Cultural Learning Centre, London, Ontario 1983; Barb Thomas, *Multiculturalism at Work: A Guide to Organized Change*: Toronto, YWCA, 1987.

11 V. Strong-Boag. *Mapping Women's Studies in Canada: Some Signposts.* **Journal of Educational Thought** 17:2, pp. 94-111, 1983; M. Boxer, *For and About Women: The Theory and Practice of Women's Studies in the United States* in N. Keohan (ed.) **Feminist Theory: A Critique of Ideology,** Chicago: University of Chicago Press, 1982.

12 M. O'Brien. **The Politics of Reproduction.** London: Routledge and Kegan Paul, 1981.

13 M. Eichler and J. Lapointe, *On the Treatment of the Sexes in Research.* Ottawa: Social Sciences and Humanities Research Council, 1985, p. 5.

14 Adrienne Rich. *Taking Women Seriously* in **On Lies Secrets and Silence,** New York: Norton 1979, pp.237-246.

15 J.R. Martin. *The Ideal of the Educated Person* in **Philosophy of Education** 1981, Daniel R. DeNicola (ed.) Illinois:Philosophy of Education Society, 1982.

16 J.R. Martin. *Reclaiming a Conversation: The Ideal of the Educated Woman.* New Haven: Yale University Press, 1985, pp. 197-8.

17 Martin, op. cit..

18 op. cit.

19 C. Gilligan. **In a Different Voice.** Cambridge: Harvard University Press.

20 M. Belenky et al. **Women's Ways of Knowing.** New York: Basic Books, 1986.

21 Myra Sadker and David Sadker. *Sexism in the Classroom: From Grade School to Graduate School.* **Phi Delta Kappa,** March 1986.

22 Mary Kay Thompson Tetreault. *It's So Opinioney,* **Journal of Education.** Vol 168, no. 2, 1986.

23 Carol Tauris and Alice Baumgartner. *How Would Your Life Be Different.*

Chapter 3

Teachers, Child-Care Workers & Mothers:

The Work of Caring and Educating

If we want to empower girls as students, we have to empower women as educators and caretakers. Otherwise, our attempts to win sex equality will be futile, for the contradictions of people working in unequal hierarchies of power will speak louder than the equality they might try to achieve for others.

Further, the empowerment of women in educating and caretaking has to proceed on two levels at the same time, just as does the fight for equal opportunity for students. As explained in the first chapter, the fight on one level is for women to be free to take courses and jobs that traditionally have belonged to men. On the other level the fight is to revalue and empower traditional women's work. Either fight is partial and futile without the other, for the end goal is a society in which women's skills and talents are accepted as valid as those of men, and equally rewarded no matter where they are employed.

The major strategy for improving the position of women teachers has been affirmative action—to ensure women equal access with men to jobs and promotions. This includes permitting and encouraging women teachers to take senior positions in educational administration. This level of the struggle has received some support from governments, school boards, teacher associations and the general public. But achieving equality for women educators also requires something broader and deeper: it requires that the value of what teachers and parents do be totally reappraised. That is the level at which some of our hardest work remains to be done. Ultimately, it includes a radical change in the way decisions are made within the educational system so that all its workers and participants have a say about how things are done.

The Need for Equal Power in Education

Although women have always taught children, their status as teachers was devalued in Canada from the start. Before the public school system was well-developed, women taught small groups of children informally in their homes and in what were known as "dame schools". Women first sought jobs in the public education system partly because they were skilled at working with children, but also because there were few other jobs outside the home available to them. And they were hired in large numbers not only because they were thought to have the mothering skills appropriate for young children, but also because they would work more cheaply than men. School boards were keen to keep down the cost of teachers' salaries, especially as the number of schools expanded much faster than the tax base in the 19th Century.[1] That was a main reason why, after public schooling became compulsory toward the end of the 1800s, women came to out-number men as teachers.

Today, over half of all Canadian teachers are women, but their participation remains largely segregated by level and rank. Women out-number men substantially in the lower grades but not in the upper grades nor in the administration of schooling. While over 70 per cent of elementary school teachers are women, about two-thirds of all high school teachers are men.[2]

Women and men also differ in the kinds of subjects they teach. In high schools men outnumber women substantially, but men are unlikely to teach home economics. In British Columbia in the 1986-87 school year, 49 men and 716 women taught home economics. Mathematics was taught by 286 women and 1,654 men, science by 219 women and 1,438 men, industrial education by 5 women and 900 men and computer education by 18 women and 215 men.[3]

In administrative positions, men vastly out-number women. This is the case even in elementary schools across Canada, where well over three-quarters of the principals and vice-principals are men and two-thirds of department heads are men. In secondary schools, about 90 per cent of the principals and vice-principals are men; about three-quarters of department heads are men. Central office administration is even more likely to be male-dominated; only 6 per cent of superintendents, for example, are women.[4]

Women teachers are under-represented in the administration not only of schools but also of teaching associations. Until very recently, very few presidents of provincial/territorial teachers' associations were women, although just under half of all executives were women.[5]

One thing these figures show is that women have less chance than men of being promoted to higher-paying administrative positions. Women thus lack the most basic kind of equal opportunity, a fact that is reflected in their salaries. In the past, women teachers and administrators received less than men even if they held the same qualifications and positions. That is no longer true; today's pay scales are the same for women and men. And yet, the average female teacher in Canada earns about $6,000 a year less than the average male.[6] Women teachers have fewer educational qualifications and are less likely to have the extra income that comes with an administrative position.

Another thing the figures show is that women have less say than men in how their schools are run, how their teaching is organized and how working conditions are set. This point has broad implications. Having less power in the schools, women quite accurately do not see themselves as co-managers or decision-makers in schooling. And quite accurately, students, parents and male teachers do not see them that way either. It would hardly be surprising, then, if women educators continued to be viewed as innately second-rate where educational administration is concerned. But the problem is deeper than the image or the prestige of women. Their exclusion from the top positions means that the extent to which women would "do it differently"—as Charol Shakeschaft and Jane Roland Martin have suggested, for example, in the previous chapter—can never be fully realized. Women's contribution to the education of both men and women is thereby curtailed.

Three Misleading Myths About Unequal Power

Why do women earn less? Why are they confined to less prestigious areas? Why do they enjoy less power and influence in the way schools are run?

The answers we give to these questions will reflect our assumptions about sex and gender, and will have a big impact on the kind of policies we propose. Some answers that are often given hold women responsible for their own lack of success. They lie in the realm of popular myth, and are often used to justify policies that maintain male dominance. Like all myths, they contains elements of truth and untruth. We need to look at them critically.

One particularly prevalent myth maintains that women bring their low status upon themselves by lack of commitment to their work, a lack caused by childbearing and rearing responsibilities. Only the male professional exhibits dedicated zeal for his work; only he can legitimately demand an administrative position and salary. Female teachers, so this argument goes, are unable to measure up to the heroism of the male professional.

If male teachers show disinterest in their work, it is assumed that something is wrong with the job: it is not challenging, it lacks upward mobility, it is alienating. If female teachers show disinterest, it is assumed that the problem lies with the "natural" prior commitment all women have to their families. The problem is much less often attributed to the way their work is organized, or to how power is distributed.[7]

This characterization is obviously wrong. Evidence shows that when women teach they are as committed to their work as men are to theirs. Women's disinterest, like men's, is likely to be caused by poor working conditions and lack of opportunity for variety and mobility in their work. Some evidence suggests, however, that women are especially bound to the ideals of serving the child's interest rather than achieving personal gain for themselves.[8]

What is true about the above myth, however, is that many women teachers (certainly not all) do have the difficult job of balancing both teaching and child-rearing responsibilities. They do not have a wife to do the homework. The "double day" that many women teachers work fits uneasily with the male standard of a single-minded career path.

Men are more likely to be promoted because they have a family to support, but women in such a situation are seen as less suited for advancement. The fault here lies in the way work—especially administrative work—is organized, in that it does not accommodate to family events and responsibilities. And the fault lies in the way homes are organized, burdening women with the double day.

A second myth suggests that women remain in lower-status positions as a result of their reluctance to make tough decisions and endure conflict. What women lack are the natural feisty and aggressive personalities of men. There is some truth in this simplistic myth. Men have for centuries aggressively excluded women from participation in teaching, educational administration and higher education, using women's childbearing duties or other supposed attributes, such as frailty or psychological timidity, to justify keeping themselves at the top. Men have proved quite effective at keeping women out of male networks of power.

But contrary to the myth of female timidity and passivity, the record shows that women—and women teachers among them—have always resisted and fought back. They have sought influence and control over their teaching lives. Their struggle to acquire higher education during the late nineteenth century in itself shows a spiritedness quite adequate to the role of decision-makers.[9] They have been denied decision-making power not because of their frailities but because of men's protection of an accumulation of power.

Yet to say that women have fought strongly against that protectionism is not to imply that women are aggressive in the same way as men. Studies of gender differences, in fact, show that women are encouraged to be more socially-sensitive than men, and that they learn to place priority on harmonious social relations, particularly in the family. But far from being a problem arising from lack of aggressiveness or ambition, these tendencies for caring are another strength that women bring to their work. Some feminists argue that women's nurturing capabilities, in fact, make them the better administrators.[10]

A third myth suggests that women teachers have positions of less influence than men because they have less education. Again, there is some truth here. In early 1970s, for example, the vast majority (72 per cent) of male educators in Canada had at least one university degree; only 36 per cent of female educators did. The lower educational achievements of women educators are in part a legacy of the past when standards were explicitly set lower for female than for male recruits to teaching. This different standard was based on the expectation that women would be confined to teaching young children (who were seen to require less skilled and educated teachers) and would not be administrators.

But the gap is closing. By 1985-86, 73 per cent of female educators had one or more degrees, compared to 90 per cent of men. In 1986, women earned 60 per cent of all masters of education degrees, and 51 per cent of all PhDs in education awarded in Canada.[11] The pool of highly-educated women has broadened to the point where numbers are not a barrier to the appointment of women administrators.

In sum, these three myths blaming women for their lower positions in teaching are wrong largely because they fail to acknowledge how systematically men have excluded women from the higher ranks.

The Inadequate Gains of Affirmative Action

The major strategy in force at the moment for ensuring women's representation in all job categories is employment equity legislation, often referred to as "affirmative action". The term employment equity was coined in Canada to avoid many of the negative associations connected with the term "affirmative action" and its implementation in the U.S. In Canada, the program does not include the explicit targets for the representation of women and minorities which were part of the programme in the United States.

Employment equity legislation recognizes that many people have been excluded from jobs for being female (or visible minorities, native people or disabled persons). It is designed to eliminate systematic discrimination by the careful monitoring of job categories to detect the unequal representation of these groups, and by ensuring that policies are in place to encourage more egalitarian hiring. It puts the responsibility on the shoulders of employers, and signals an end to the simplistic blaming of marginalized groups for their lack of participation.

But the federal employment equity legislation does not cover boards of education, and most provinces do not have similar legislation. Employment equity programs have only recently been applied to schools; they are high on the agenda of teachers' associations in Canada, but only a few provinces have started them at the board level.

The Ontario Ministry of Education in 1986 provided incentive funding for affirmative action and requested school boards to start programs "with the aim of raising the number and diversifying the occupational distribution of women to a minimum of 30 per cent in all occupational categories by the year 2000."[12] The policy has had a good effect. Between 1986 and 1988, while the proportion of female applicants to positions of responsibility stayed at 46 per cent, the number actually appointed to those posts rose from 49 to 63 per cent.[13]

Yet the Ontario Minister of Education acknowledged in April 1989 that many more women must be appointed before employment equity is achieved. As of September 1990 the Ministry of

Education will require (not just encourage) school boards to enact employment policies for women and to appoint senior officials to enforce them. The minimum objective for representation by women in positions of responsibility will be raised to 50 per cent by the year 2000.[14]

Other provinces have been reluctant to take such steps. At best, they've offered nice suggestions but little more. British Columbia's Royal Commission on Education in 1988 proposed that hiring and promotion practices be free from gender bias and be equitable to all. The commission recommended that the education ministry "monitor and report" data annually on matters such as the percentages of female counsellors and administrators in the schools.[15] Such recommendations, vague as they are, have yet to be implemented by the government.

In Nova Scotia, three "major partners in education" started an affirmative action program in 1988. They are the Minister of Education, the president of the teachers' union, and the president of the school boards' association. These three partners urged school boards to review hiring procedures. They recommended "an equitable distribution of the sexes at all levels of decision-making, consistent with the size of the district school board staff, and the designation of a senior official to the distribution board to report regularly on the affirmative action program."[16] But their proposals had no teeth; they were only recommendations.

Such policy proposals may help to identify the problem, but they are too vague to provide solutions. They do not spell out how the reviews should be done, what the equity goals should be, and what pressure could be brought upon the educational system to ensure that affirmative action is practiced. Such policies can easily coexist with a reluctance to act.

Objections to Affirmative Action

The objections most frequently raised against affirmative action have to do with the possible preference and additional power that this would give to women, and an apprehension about what they would do with this power. Again, as with the myths used to rationalize women's exclusion from the top jobs, these objections are mixed with half-truths and fears that need to be carefully sorted out.

One objection is that this affirmative action would result in women being hired who are less capable than men. Some think it would give women an advantage over men. But this is just not so. It only means that men should no longer be given, because of sex, a head-start over women. It acknowledges that men have been given advantages over women that they must now relinquish.

Affirmative action does not mean always hiring a woman when a top management position becomes vacant. It means working towards a more equal representation of women in positions from which they have been excluded. It is based on the premise that women are as competent as men, and if given the opportunity to display that competence, they will perform better than men who had been given such positions because of their sex. Affirmative action does not displace the necessity of making difficult judgments with an arbitrary criterion of gender. But it does mean that we can no longer pretend that hiring decisions are sex-blind; it insists on taking sex and gender explicitly into account.

Another objection to affirmative action programmes rests on the belief that when women gain positions of power they will simply push for "women's issues". This objection is based on a number of false assumptions, one of them being that men don't push for "men's issues." Another is the assumption that "women's issues" somehow fail to be basically human issues, that they are a world apart from essential human concerns. To fall into that confusion is to essentialize sex, to define women as a unified class that shares a set of shared intersts that are quite different from those of men, instead of recognizing that wide variations exist among both women and men.

Sex and gender do, however, organize our lives, and does mean that men and women have different experiences. There is some truth in the assumption that women would press for other solutions to human problems. Because of their greater involvement in nurturing tasks, women administrators may be more inclined than men administrators to define teaching in ways that go beyond intellectual development into the realm of social and personal development. Because of their sex, women may also be more inclined to recognize the importance of understanding women's history, women's achievements, and women's struggles. Perhaps they may be more willing than men to acknowledge the need to integrate women's studies into the school curriculum, and to see that a "feminist pedagogy" would enhance learning for all students.[17]

But when women gain a legitimate share of power they do not always push for women's interests, nor do they necessarily exercise more nurturing abilities than men and do a better job. When women get power and often act as badly as men who have power, it should come as no surprise. What is at issue is that women should have the same rights as men to exercise power.

Affirmative action is about increasing the representation of groups that have been systematically denied access to power. It is about assessing competence, about allowing people to acquire power on the basis of what they can do, not who they are.

Employment equity programmes therefore need to be strengthened, encouraged and expanded. They need to cover employees in all areas of the school system—caretakers, secretaries and cafeteria workers—not just teachers and administrators. They need to monitor the job prospects of native people, visible minorities, and disabled people, as well as women.

What Kind of Power Do We Want?

There is another objection to affirmative action, apart from those above, that we think is crucial. It is that an exclusive emphasis on equal access implies an acceptance of existing relations of value and power.

Affirmative action by itself focusses on the limited question of "who" gets power. It does not deal with the broader question of "what kind" of power is exercised and sought. It does not question how power has come to be concentrated in particular positions and how these positions have been defined as powerful. The strategy of equal access suggests only that some women should replace some men as managers of that power. We believe that such a narrow emphasis is likely to end up working against rather than for women. It is likely to divide women further—with some wielding more power and most others being left disempowered.

The affirmative action approach can end up putting an undeserved or vaunted premium on the tasks of some women while devaluing the tasks of other women. The work of mothers, secretaries, and elementary school teachers may continue to be disdained by the system as inferior to those of the principal, the superintendent and the university professor. Such an approach by itself can end up suggesting that being a teacher, mother or secretary is not good enough and never will be.

An affirmative action approach accepts a hierarchy of power that needs to be questioned and changed. The power of centralized authorities over local schools and local communities limits democratic consultation. Such a concentration of power rests on an assumed hierarchy of worth; it assumes that those at the top are much more capable of formulating policy and making decisions than those at the bottom. This hierarchical arrangement denies the possibility of broadly-based consultations taking place. It drastically limits the involvement of students, parents and teachers in deciding how schools are run. It limits how girls and women influence their conditions of learning, caring and teaching.

By itself affirmative action as a strategy doesn't address the question of value. It takes for granted the current arrangement of jobs and their supposed worth. It assumes that certain jobs deserve unquestionably more rewards, more recognition, and more ability to exercise power than other jobs. This means that the high-status jobs that some men hold are believed to be inherently more valuable than women's jobs. This belief is held within a patriarchal society, a society structured by male domination. As men, especially those of the ruling class, accumulate power, they ensure that their activities are defined as valuable relative to those of women. Their beliefs of value are held within a society that is strongly structured by a meritocratic ideology. This ideology justifies the fact that only a few (men of the ruling class) are highly rewarded and able to wield considerable power.

These are some reasons why a revaluing of "women's work" and the democratizing of the educational system needs to be pursued along with affirmative action.

Devaluing Women's Skills

What is "women's work" really worth? It is hard to get a clear picture of that because of the many ways it has been devalued in male society. This is especially true of women who work as mothers, as child-care workers, and as teachers.

The devaluation of women's educational work can be seen most simply in the wage differentials. Since a mother's work does not receive a wage, it is invisible in economic terms. The teaching of children by women is not counted in the GNP unless it is done by a paid babysitter, teacher, or daycare worker. Women's work in the two-parent home is counted in the public sphere as a mere part of the male breadwinner's upkeep. Women's work in that way is incorporated in the operation of families, and by and large taken for granted. When mothers do work outside the home their work is often like what they do in the home, and they are forced to accept jobs that pay them less than men. These wage differentials are based partly on the assumptions that a man's wage can support a family, that women's earnings are needed only for minor or frivolous expenses, and that caring for people, being the natural duty of women, demands only minimal skills and deserves only minimal rewards.

Like the work of mothers, the work of child-care workers is devalued. The federal *Task Force on Child Care* reported that in 1984 workers in daycare centres in British Columbia earned only 64 per cent of the average weekly earnings of all industries. And in Quebec, where their wages were higher than in other regions, their wage level still amounted to only 74 per cent of the average industrial wage in that province. The earnings of care-givers who look after other people's children in their own homes were even lower. Their average earnings, based on a survey by the *Task Force on Child Care*, were $3.50 an hour ($7,722 a year) in 1984.[18]

In the field of teaching, the devaluation of women's work has to do more with the lack of authority and respect than salary. Since World War II, women teachers have achieved salaries matching those of men doing the same jobs. Elementary teachers' pay scales have become equal to those of secondary teachers, and because of hard collective bargaining the salaries of all teachers have been raised to respectable levels.

The fact that women teachers' work has been afforded greater value attests to the possibility that women's work can be "revalued". But in a male-dominated class society, it would be inadequate merely to bring the value of women's work up to that of men who are doing the same work. We need also to question the persistence of the underlying occupational segregation of women's and men's work and the accompanying undervaluing of women's work.

The devaluation of the work of the teacher (who is more often than not a woman) in relation to that of an administrator (more often than not a man) is important. When educational changes are proposed, administrators are consulted more often than teachers: those farthest from the classroom have the resources and time to make sure they are heard. This leaves classroom teachers feeling unable to control the environment in which they teach.

Child-care and educational work that is largely carried out by women is caught up in the contradictory rhetoric of a society that stresses the importance of children but which devalues and underpays the care and raising of children. Yet respecting classroom teaching remains the best way to ensure good education for children. And respecting the work that mothers do in the home remains the best way to ensure that children are well cared for and educated outside the classroom.

Establishing Equal Value

As worthy as the struggle for equal pay for equal work has been, its rewards have been limited even in its success. As a result of teachers' collective struggles, for example, women did win the right to be paid equally with men doing the same kind of work, and pay differences came to rest on differences in training and seniority. But though equal pay for equal work among teachers has been largely achieved, the fight for equal pay for work of equal value has not. Men tend to manage while women tend to teach, and managers are rewarded more than teachers. Women educators, as a result, continue to be paid less than men educators, and to have less power in deciding how things should be done.

As noted above, getting a clear picture in a male society of what women's educational work is really worth is difficult. The strategy of "equal value" or pay equity is one way to go about answering this question. It carries women's struggle for equality beyond mere "equal pay for equal work" and pushes for "equal pay for work of equal value."

The strategy of "equal value" has more transformative potential than the fight to get women into "men's" jobs or to achieve equal pay for the same jobs. As Abella argues, "Why should women be asked to change their choices, rather than asking society to change how it rewards those choices?"[19] More women in diverse types of jobs are likely to benefit from equal value. As a strategy it is less likely to assume that things men do are superior, for it questions how criteria of value that reflect men's interests and activities have been applied to work. It questions the nature of the meritocratic ordering of jobs based on male criteria. Under this strategy, the skilled nature and the importance of the work women have done has a chance to be accorded value and respect while women have a chance of being consulted and empowered.

The strategy of equal value has been adopted in various ways by the federal government and several provinces in what is known as "pay equity" legislation. But this strategy has not been widely applied. It has not been used directly in the case of child-care workers or teachers and has been applied only infrequently to other school board employees, in part because of the cost.

In 1981, the Canadian Union of Public Employees (CUPE) took more than 11,000 workers, which included school board workers, in British Columbia's Lower Mainland out on strike for up to 15 weeks to back their demand for equal pay for work of equal value. The strike was settled largely in favour of CUPE but the Greater Vancouver Regional District refused to acknowledge the equal value principle.[20]

Ontario school boards, as Morna Ballantyne notes, have promoted affirmative action for non-teaching women, but because of the cost, have diligently avoided the broader measure of equal value.[21]

Despite obstacles to the idea of equal value, and perhaps because of them, teachers need to take up this strategy. They need to question the idea that the work of administrators is somehow more worthy of reward than that of teachers, that male activities are more important than female activities, and that value can be determined and measured fairly within the existing hierarchies of power.

Equal pay for work of equal value challenges these assumptions. It suggests that the hierarchical structure of teaching, and the procedures that assign more value to positions of management than to teaching, must be examined and questioned. Teachers need to ask why teaching is not as well remunerated and respected as administrative work, and decide whether the arguments for that difference make sense. If children are the business of schools, does it stand to reason that those who work most directly with them receive lower pay and have less influence?

The ways that administrative work is organized must also be held up to scrutiny. Administrative posts might be made temporary ones, so that many teachers had an opportunity to be administrators. In most cases, when a teacher becomes an administrator in the public school system, she or he remains an administrator until retirement. This separates teachers and administrators more distinctly that they are separated in the university system, where administrative appointments are temporary. The point is that revaluing reaches into the heart of how our schools are organized, how worth is established, and who has a say in how society is run.

The determination of value needs to be contested, to be negotiated. It should not rest on traditional male values and power. And it should not rest on a tightly-controlled hierarchy. Not only does women's work need to be accorded value and respect; women also need to be consulted about the assigning of value.

Once equal value is accepted as a strategy worth pursuing, the next questions are where and how to pursue it. The critical mechanism for achieving equal pay for equal value is through job evaluation. The aim is to develop gender-neutral job evaluation schemes to determine and compare the value of female and male dominated occupations, without reference to the sex of the job holder. Rather than assuming that we all know what the value of a job is, evaluation schemes open up the question. Opening up the question shows how complex the process is, how much is at stake, and how much has been taken for granted. It allows for the possibility that female activities will be accorded proper value.

Several criteria such as skills, effort, responsibility and working conditions are used to determine the value of work. Each of these criteria have to be evaluated. Decisions have to be made about what constitutes skill, how skills are to be weighted and so on. Job evaluation requires a detailed knowledge of what the job entails, and of how bias can enter into the evaluation process itself.

Job evaluation schemes are fraught with questions of value as they should be. Values enter into all stages of the process. Caring for children, for example, can be viewed as an overwhelming responsibility, as entirely unproblematic, or just literally "shit-work". How such work is evaluated will depend on who is consulted and what their values are. Job evaluation makes this process public and open to contestation, if not entirely devoid of male, class and racial biases.

Job evaluation procedures are complex, but not impossible to do. They are ideally suited for bureaucratic organizations such as schools. And teacher associations are an ideal place to press the issue of equal value.

Women teachers have an advantage over other women in this struggle because they work within well-organized associations and clearly-defined employment structures that lend themselves to job evaluation schemes. Their fight for equal value could benefit not only women teachers, but also other women who care for and educate children. Mothers and child-care workers have a much harder time—for both ideological and organizational reasons—asserting the value of their tasks.

Many people acknowledge that caring for children is a very important task, much more important than producing yet another type of car, hamburger or kitchen gadget. But in Canadian society a strong ideology maintains that child care is a "natural" duty not requiring skill and not comparable to other types of work. Another difficulty in organizing for change is that child care, very often done in the home, whether by mother or child-care worker, is not readily amenable to bureaucratic job evaluation schemes for achieving equal pay for equal value. Even the managers of day-care centres (who are almost exclusively women) are poorly paid in comparison with other types of managers. But even though it is difficult and complex, equal value legislation for child care is necessary. With the future of our children at stake, such work cannot continue to be so grossly undervalued. The kinds of skill, effort and responsibility that the work entails must be recognized. This recognition must be translated into better pay, more respect and more influence.

The point is that the work of teachers, child-care workers and mothers is all directed toward the same ends. These types of work are similarly executed and devalued. Thus, strategies of revaluation could be applied to all three types of child care and educative work (as well as other types of caring such as nursing and social work) to enhance the value of childwork all around. Ideally, a broad coalition of all these groups would take on this challenge.

Winning Back Power

The extent to which equal value legislation changes things depends on how thoroughly it is pursued. As a strategy, equal value cannot just be about equal pay. It has to be about the broader issues of respect and influence. Pay is obviously important for giving the teacher value. But ultimately teachers and educators need to have control over their work, to have a sense of overall purpose in what they are doing, to influence the conditions of their work, and to help decide how children are to be taught.

Equal value is not just about designing a more efficient meritocracy so that value is based on gender-neutral criteria. It is not about elevating the teacher as expert, inadvertently adding to the devaluation of mothering. It is about being more inclusive in the definition of value, respecting the work of more people and consulting with them more fully as decisions are made.

Teachers and Mothers Together

The devaluation of the work of mothers in relation to the work of professionals is an issue that is generally ignored by educators. It shouldn't be. The devaluation of women's educational work includes work done by mothers at home with their children, and the fight against devaluation has to include them.

Teaching has often been defined as making up for inadequacies of the home—meaning the mother, especially the poor mother. Research on the home-school relationship often focusses on how the cultures of specific types of families (e.g. working class, immigrant, native) deprive children of advantages that are taken for granted by the educational system. This research makes little reference to the work of mothers in its abstracted references to families, but it is mothers who do the work. It indirectly blames mothers for any failures in their children but takes the schools' and their own work for granted.[22]

Obviously, researchers who approach their work this way are looking at it from the point of view of the educational system, not from that of mothers. Their research does not usually ask how women's work is shaped by the schools, how child-rearing is influenced by educational pedagogy, how both teaching and mothering are affected by changing educational resources, or how sex and gender affect the work of both teachers and mothers. They fail to consider how the relationships between mothers and teachers are shaped by social class, ethnicity and patriarchal structures, as well as by gender. And so, partly by default, the relationship of mothers and teachers has been defined as antagonistic.[23]

Instead of all that, we need to look at the structures that marginalize and devalue both mothers and teachers. Cutbacks in the resources available to schools, for example, increase the demands placed on both mothers and teachers. They both have to work harder with fewer rewards when the state renegs on its obligations. Coalitions of parents and teachers need to join forces in fighting the devaluation of educational work, for it affects both home and school, both mother and teacher.

Conclusion

To improve the position of female educators, several strategies are necessary. Equal access—ensuring that women are given an equal chance with men for hiring and promotion—is useful for several reasons. It can advance the careers of individual women, it can enable more women to have an impact on how schools are run, and it makes available more positive role models for female students.

But we have seen that by itself the strategy of equal access is limited. The strategy of equal value has much more potential to transform the ordinary work of caring and educating children. It is intended to accord respect, power and dignity as well as monetary rewards to the work of teachers, child-care workers and mothers.

Giving value to the work of caring and educating is essential, but the way the work is organized and carried out must be changed in order to accomplish this. Teachers must insist on having a fair share of power in deciding how they do their work as educators, not leaving it wholly to the "experts," the ministries of education and the educational administrators. Those who do the work of caring and educating need to build coalitions that give strength to their demands for the revaluing of their labour.

FOOTNOTES

[1] Marta Danylewycz, Beth Light and Alison Prentice, *The Evolution of the Sexual Division of Labour in Teaching: Nineteenth Century Ontario and Quebec Case Study,* in Jane Gaskell and Arlene McLaren, **Women and Education: A Canadian Perspective**. Calgary: Detselig, 1987.

[2] Statistics Canada, *Characteristics of Teachers in Public Elementary and Secondary Schools 1985-86.* Ottawa: Minister of Supply and Services, 1987, Table 1.

[3] Marian Dodds and Lisa Pedrini. **Rights of Girls and Women in Education**. Vancouver: B.C. Teachers' Federation, Dec. 1987, p. 2.

[4] Statistics Canada. *Characteristics of Teachers 1985-86* , Table 1.

[5] Linda MacLeod. *Progess as Paradox: Will Women teachers Build Tomorrow?* Presented to the Canadian Teachers' Federation, Tenth National Conference on the Status of Women and Education, November

10, 1988, p. 4.

6 **Ibid,** p. 2.

7 For a similar analysis of women's work in general see Roslyn L. Feldberg and Evelyn Nanano Glenn. *Male and Female: Job Versus Gender Models in the Sociology of Work* in Rachel Kahn-Hut et al. **Women and Work: Problems and Perspectives.** New York: Oxford University Press, 1982.

8 Sari Knopp Biklen. *Can Elementary Schoolteaching Be a Career?: A Search for New Ways of Understanding Women's Work.* **Issues in Education,** III (3), 1985.

9 For an account of women's struggles to gain entry to McGill University, see Margaret Gillett. **We Walked Very Warily: A History of Women at McGill.** Montreal: Eden Press Women's Publications, 1981.

10 Charol Shakeshaft. *A Gender at Risk.* **Phi Delta Kappan,** March 1986.

11 Linda MacLeod, *Progress as Paradox,* p. 3.

12 Federation of Women Teachers' Associations of Ontario. *Affirmative Action Report 1987.* Toronto, p. 1.

13 Toronto Board of Education. *Summary of Data Gathering–Teaching Staff,* July 1, 1987 to June 30, 1988.

14 Donn Downey. *Minister Pledges Job Equity in Education.* **The Globe and Mail,** April 1, 1989.

15 The Honourable Anthony J. Brummet, *Policy Directions: A Response to the Sullivan Royal Commission on Education by the Government of British Columbia.* Vancouver: Minister of Education, Province of British Columbia, January 27, 1989, p. 23.

16 The Honourable Ronald C. Giffin, Karen Willis Duerden and Reid MacVicar, *A Joint Statement on the Employment of Women in Education.* Nova Scotia: March 1988.

17 Charol Shakeshaft. *A Gender at Risk.*

18 Task Force on Child Care. *Report on the Task Force on Child Care* Ottawa: Minister of Supply and Services, 1986, Chapter 5.

19 Cited in Heather E. Conway. *Equal Pay for Work of Equal Value Legislation in Canada: An Analysis.* Ottawa: **Studies in Social Policy,** November 1987, p. 5.

20 Conway. *Equal Pay for Work of Equal Value,* p. 21.

21 Morna Ballantyne. *Missing the Mark for Women Workers: Affirmative Action in Ontario School Boards,* **Our Schools/Our Selves,** 1 (3), 1989.

Chapter 4

Post-Secondary Education and Beyond

In the previous chapters we primarily examined the application of the feminist agenda to primary and secondary education. We looked at several strategies that are employed or could be employed to strive for gender equity in the public school sector. In this chapter we will point to ways in which the same issues are important in other forms of education—post-secondary education, adult education, and the informal learning we all do every day. And in summing up feminist issues for educators, we want to ground them in the political objectives of a broad democratic socialist politics.

Equal Opportunity

As we have stressed earlier, equal educational opportunity for girls and women includes equal access to what is available to boys and men: equal access to subjects in the physical sciences and mathematics, to higher education, to higher paying jobs, to power, to respect and to learning. The struggle to achieve this equality continues at all levels of education but particularly at the higher levels.

For decades the under-representation of women at universities as undergraduates was the most striking index of women's educational deficits. In 1920, women were 16% of undergraduate students in Canada. In 1950, they were 21%. By 1970, they were barely 35%.[1]

Since 1970, however, the number of women enrolled in universities as undergraduates has climbed dramatically. Today, more than one-half of full-time undergraduates are women. At community colleges, women are even more highly represented than at universities.

But inequality remains on other significant measures of postsecondary achievement: the proportion of graduate degrees obtained, the segregation of the sexes in specific fields, and job outcomes. The higher the level of degree, the less likely women are to participate. In 1984-85 just over one-quarter of all those who obtained doctorates in Canada were women, and most of their degrees were in "women's fields".[2]

In all types of post-secondary education, men dominate in certain fields, women in others. At the community colleges, women are over-represented in education and health fields but under-represented in the fields of transportation, technologies, and natural resources. In 1982-83, only 10% of college diplomas in the field of technologies were awarded to women. At universities women are over represented in such fields as education, household science and nursing, but under-represented in fields like the physical sciences, engineering and commerce. In 1984-85 only 27% of bachelor degrees in the physical sciences were awarded to women; the proportion awarded in engineering was even lower at 10%.

Those areas in which women concentrate are growing more slowly, receive less research funding, and lead to lower paying jobs than those areas in which men predominate. This type of segregation means that women are personally disadvantaged. It also means they are less able to exercise influence on how things happen in the world.

Yet the concentration of women in certain fields is changing. Between 1970-71 and 1984-85 the proportion of women rose dramatically in medicine from 15% to 38%, in commerce from 6% to 38%, in law from 9% to 42%.[3] Change is possible. Segregation is not natural or inevitable, but socially-produced.

Measures have been introduced by the federal government, provincial governments, professional associations and universities to increase women's access to post-secondary education. In 1988, the federal government promised to spend $40-million in five years to produce more women scientists and engineers. At least half of a total of 2500 Canada scholarships to support undergraduate science students are to go to women. Some universities have set up review committees to suggest ways to improve women's access. A 1985 report at the University of Toronto for example recommended that:

> The university should develop an active program of recruiting young women to non-traditional programs, creating new recruitment materials (as have been done by the University of Waterloo for the field of engineering), establishing positions with specific responsibilities for liaison with high schools, and sponsoring career workshops in secondary schools to make young women aware of career options and their academic requirements.[4]

The problem of women's unequal access to non-traditional fields and opportunities is, nevertheless, often neglected. A 1988 British Columbia report concerned with promoting access to advanced education and job training, focussed on several under-represented groups (native Indians, people in small remote communities and the disabled), but neglected to include women.[5]

Education continues well beyond public schooling. Adult education and training are particularly important to women, as the

Royal Commission on the Status of Women noted almost twenty years ago:

> Because of accelerating technological change, learning more than ever before is regarded as a continuing process throughout life. In the past, educational instititions, engrossed in the education of the young, were slow to acknowledge the potential as well as the special problem of adults, while today they are aware of the need to encompass and encourage mature students. Women who have been "only a housewife" and now see a new way of life and women and men whose jobs have been altered or eliminated are taking advantage of a second chance for education.6

Recent studies have suggested that women out-number men in adult education classes. One survey in 1983 found that 56% of adult learners were women. But, as in all other kinds of education, women's learning opportunities here are concentrated in different fields from men's. Women dominate in hobby/craft/recreation courses (80%), in personal development/general interest courses (66%), and in academic courses (56%). They are under-represented in job-related courses (39%).7

Even when women are in vocational courses, they are less likely than men to have their fees paid by their employers. One study found that 35% of men's training, but only 14% of women's training is paid for by their employers.8 Women are less likely to be in vocational courses because they are less likely to be in jobs where employers will sponsor them. Women's jobs have flatter career lines and less on-the-job training than men's jobs. Women constitute about one-quarter to one-third of those enrolled in federally-supported vocational training programs. The level of female enrolment in national training programs has declined since 1977-78. Women's share of places in General Industrial Training declined from 28% in 1977-78 to 24% in 1983-84, while their share of spaces in full-time institutional training dropped from 32% to 27.5%. The proportion of women in apprenticeship programmes is much smaller. In 1983-84 only 4% of apprentices who began full-time courses under the institutional training programmewere women.

Within vocational training itself, gender segregation is strong. Under the institutional training program in 1984-85, women made up 93% of the trainees in clerical occupations but only 5% of those in construction occupations. The only blue-collar job for which large numbers of women train is sewing machine operator.[9]

Groups such as CCLOW (Canadian Congress for Learning Opportunities for Women) and CAAE-ICEA (Canadian Association for Adult Education and l'Institut Canadien d'Education des Adultes) have lobbied the government on many issues related to women's participation in adult education: inadequate training allowances (especially for those women with children), low unemployment insurance benefits (since women earn lower wages on average than men), training in "surplus" occupations (those in which there is an excess supply of labour in local labour markets such as clerical work), scarcity of child care, lack of affirmative action strategies and the need for aggressive recruitment campaigns.

This stress on women's low participation rate in non-traditional educational and training programs in universities, colleges and adult education programs is important. Women need greater access to male-dominated fields. They need to have the same chance as men to be educated in the fields of engineering, technologies and construction. They need to have an equal chance to obtain jobs that are highly skilled and valued. But this emphasis on equal access to male-dominated fields begs the question of *equal access to what?* What is the content of the courses women are seeking access to? Do the courses (in traditional as well as non-traditional fields) and the ways they are organized reflect women's experiences and ways of knowing?

Equal Form, Equal Content

Educators must not just assume that treating girls the same way that boys have always been treated constitutes equality for women. As Dale Spender argues:

> When the aim is to provide women with exactly the same education as men there is an underlying assumption that

the male way is the right way, and that one of the solutions to women's oppression lies in having women receive an equal share of the fruits of the ostensibly superior male educational diet . . . Women have played virtually no part in determining the shape and form of education in our society. The models of education were firmly established and were within male control before women began their fight to enter educational institutions. Those models of education are still formulated and controlled by males.[10]

The form that the post-secondary sector takes must be changed to accommodate women. Besides recruiting women to non-traditional programs, universities and colleges must provide greater financial and organizational support to women. In the 1985 University of Toronto report cited earlier, the different experiences of women and men were recognized. Recommendations focussed on such problems for women as the lack of financial aid for students in arts and humanities programs as opposed to the sciences; the loss of graduate fellowships as a result of parental leave; the need for a part-time Ph.D. status to enable mothers to continue with their graduate studies; the necessity of improved child-care services on campus; and the need for more programmes and opportunities to attract and serve mature women.

As this report suggests, women's interests in the arts and humanities need financial support, and their distinctive experiences as mothers and their interrupted career patterns need recognition and organizational support. Women should not be treated as if they were all the same age or had the same life experiences. Nor should their educational programmes be modelled on those of men.

A striking example of problems faced by female students is sexual harassment. Recently, groups of concerned students and faculty in many universities and colleges across Canada have pressured their administrations to develop policies that acknowledge and deal with the problem of sexual harassment on campus. Despite strong resistance from many members of the academic community, such policies have been established and implemented on campuses across Canada.

Accomodating the post-secondary sector to women is not,

however, just a matter of improving financial and organizational support. It also means that the curriculum and how things are taught must be changed. As in primary and secondary school curriculum, women tend to be either absent or stereotyped in post-secondary curriculum. In the discipline of sociology, for example, women's lives are highlighted in studies of family life but are eclipsed in the study of other realms in society. Students are likely to learn about the problem of unwed mothers, but not about the problem of unwed fathers. They are likely to learn about the political participation of men, but not of women.

What is taught in universities and colleges is obviously important. These are the sites where higher learning takes place and where future teachers are trained. But even more fundamentally, these institutions don't just transmit knowledge, they produce it. But who produces it?

Many feminists have noted that women have been largely excluded from the process of producing and creating ideas. Scholarship has largely been dominated by men. In her influential article written in 1975, Dorothy Smith refers to the "circle effect":

> Men attend to and treat as significant only what men say. The circle of men whose writing and talk was significant to each other extends backwards in time as far as our records reach. What men were doing was relevant to men, was written by men about men for men. Men listened and listen only to what one man says to another. A tradition is formed in this discourse of the past within the present. The themes, problematics, assumptions, metaphors, and images are formed as the circle of those present draws upon the work of the past. From this circle women have been to a large extent excluded. They have been admitted to it only by special licence and as individuals, not as representatives of their sex. They can share in it only by receiving its terms and relevances and these are the terms and relevances of a discourse among men. [1]

Through routine practices of socialization, education, work and communication patterns, women have been excluded. At best, they have received ideas; they have rarely participated in their creation. As a result of being excluded from the circle of properly authorized speakers and hearers, women's activities don't count. A minus factor is attached to the woman novelist, woman physicist, woman engineer.

Dorothy Smith argues that in a world that is socially constructed by men, women appear as objects. Women's experiences and consciousness are not seen as the origin of knowledge–an authoritative perspective on the world–as are men's. Women don't set standards, produce social knowlege, or act as gatekeepers over what is admitted as knowledge and as worthwhile.

What men have thought, what they have considered to be important has come to be accepted as objective and universally true. Their own particular experiences and perspectives are not made transparent. Women, Smith argues, must scrutinize this knowledge base from the perspective of women's experiences and interests.

And feminists have done just that. They have launched massive attacks on all disciplines of knowledge, for all of them reveal male-oriented questions and assumptions. In talking about male biases in political sociology, Thelma McCormack's analogy helps to capture the problem:

> The most flagrant biases are...: inability to empathize with women, lack of knowledge about women generally, and the absence of information dealing specifically with women's political experience...As things now stand in our data banks, we have male-female differences to questions men have raised arising out of their own or other men's experience. It is as if one attempted to understand rural life by having engineers ask farmers their opinions about traffic congestion.[12]

As noted in the previous chapter, in 1985 Margrit Eichler and Jeanne Lapointe published a widely distributed pamphlet that reveals many of the ways that traditional scholarship is male-biased. More recently, Eichler has provided a more thorough analysis of this problem.[13] She identifies seven sexist problems in research ranging from androcentricity (a view of the world from a male perspective) to double standards (when identical behaviours or situations of women and men are evaluated, treated or measured by different criteria).

Androcentricity is revealed in many of the standard concepts used by social scientists. A recent article defines "intergroup warfare" as "a means of gaining women and slaves." Women are "gained". And for whom are they gained? For men, of course. Men, not women, are conceptualized as group members. Such an analysis begs many questions. Did women engage in intergroup warfare or was it solely a male activity? What were women doing if they weren't engaged in intergroup warfare? What were the relationships among the women of the different groups?

Double standards in the use of language, concepts, and research instruments are also common practice in research. Non-parallel terms for males and females in parallel situations are used. Until recently, no one thought to question the expression "man and wife". For equal treatment of the sexes the expression should be "man and woman" or "husband and wife". This still leaves the question of order and the implied value of importance in placing men first. To be fully equal, the expression should be "woman and man" and "wife and husband" as much as the other way around.

Feminists are not just scrutinizing traditional "malestream" knowledge for its male bias. They are also trying to develop women-centred perspectives and research. As Eichler reminds us, this is not easy. Such an attempt occurs within an overall intellectual environment that has been coloured for years by androcentric thinking. But increasingly women are producing ideas that stem from women's experiences and perceptions and that challenge entrenched views. From their experiences, women have insisted that rape is not just a sexual offence, but an assault. They have "discovered" the existence of sexual harassment and its threatening implications for women. Women have discovered that families are not necessarily havens for them.

With the rise of feminist scholarship the presence of women in the university curriculum has improved. Women writers and scientists are being discussed, questions especially relevant to women such as family violence and abortion are being addressed.

Women students are increasingly able to pursue topics that are of direct interest to them. Their lives and those of their mothers, aunts, grandmothers, and women they never knew are being addressed by academic scholarship. The so-called "objectivity" of the academic disciplines is being called into question as are their traditional debates and questions.

But the institutional support for such endeavours is very slim indeed, limiting the impact of feminist scholarship and curriculum on universities.

Some universities and colleges have begun to develop policies to encourage gender-neutral language on their campuses. In a recent survey carried out by the Association of Universities and Colleges of Canada, five of the reporting universities had formal policies on gender-neutral language. However, as yet none had a policy regarding gender-neutral curriculum.[14]

Still, feminist scholarship is having an impact on the method and content of the disciplines through women's studies courses as well as through the integration of women's experiences into traditional courses. Most universities have some type of women's studies programme. They are usually poorly-funded with few faculty attached. But given the high level of commitment of women's studies students and faculty, they have had a considerable impact. As a result of the creation of five endowed chairs by the Secretary of State in 1985, a few women's studies programmes across Canada have become more secure.

Women's studies programmes are especially helpful in giving legitimation and visibility to the academic study of women's experiences and institutional support for feminist students and scholars. At Simon Fraser University, for example, graduate students and faculty of the women's studies programme meet regularly as a group to discuss their research, to attend talks of invited speakers and so on.

A circle has been created where women speak to and hear one another. As noted in the previous chapter, the creation of women's studies programmes risks ghettoization. But because these programmes are essential for allowing women to become authorities on their own experiences and knowledge, the risk is worth taking.

Much more dangerous for women is the resistance on campuses to feminist scholarship. Based on male norms, decisions have been made that deny feminist scholars appointments, tenure and promotion. University committees use criteria of "excellence" that subtly discrimintate against feminist work.[15] The guise of academic freedom has not protected feminist research and publishing. Such research has been underfunded by research agencies and under-published in academic journals and presses.

Despite the resistance, women's studies programmes have continued to develop and universities are increasingly integrating women's experiences into their courses. Feminist research and publications have burgeoned. Some mainstream publishers are responding to the high demand in this field and women's presses have been developed to produce books and journals about women.

The creation and dissemination of feminist scholarship plays a pivotal role in the educational equality of women and the educational enrichment of men. Above all, feminist scholarship offers a political and scholarly standpoint from which to imagine and build a transformed academy and society.

But what is a woman's standpoint? In revaluing and incorporating the female experience we must not romanticize women's culture or draw on one privileged part of it while neglecting the rest. Reshaping educational institutions means making them more permeable, more responsive to people of many different backgrounds, more able to respond to the particular exigencies of lives lived in differing ethnic, racial, class, age and sexual communities. Within women's scholarship, a central question has become how to include the diversity of women's experience, how to both hold on to the categories of gender, and at the same time transform them, by recognizing the diversity within them. Most women suffer not only from male bias in the curriculum but also from class, racial or ethnic biases. Feminist scholarship must include the study of women's experiences as they are lived out in historically and socially-specific ways.

For over a decade the problem of access to adult education and job training programmes has claimed much of the attention of feminists concerned about this sector of women's education. More recently a focus on the content and pedagogy of such programs has begun to emerge. Informed by feminist critiques of the curriculum in other educational sectors and also by radical adult educators such as Paulo Freire,[16] the main concern of this analysis is with the male-biased nature of knowledge and pedagogy and how it can be transformed to revalue women's experiences.

This strategy to revalue women's experiences by transforming the curriculum and methods of teaching can build upon some of the strengths of the adult education movement and programs. Adult education has had a long history of being concerned with inequality and "really useful knowledge". Furthermore, it is not so constrained by the rigidities and political control of the regular educational school system. If we are to believe its rhetorical claims, it is flexible in response to student needs, it emphasizes empowerment, and it has non-hierarchical structures.

When feminists do organize the education of adult women, evidence suggests that they are inclined to develop a new type of education: one that is less authoritarian, centred on learning rather than teaching, and one that includes women's experiences, and transforms the curriculum.

Women as Educational Workers

As noted in Chapter Three, to promote women's education, it is necessary to promote women as teachers. This involves affirmative action when it comes to promotion and to hiring administrators. But it also involves revaluing what teachers and administrators do, acknowledging the importance of the kinds of teaching and research that women have undertaken.

The work of women educators needs to be respected for the hard and skilled work that it is. Those who carry out the work need control over what they do, and need to have their voices heard in decisions to alter policy and organization. Their work should not be ghettoized; it should not be devalued.

Statistics on women's representation among post-secondary faculty show that fewer than one in five university faculty members are women. Between 1970-71 and 1984-85 the percentage of women faculty members increased only 4%, from 13% to 17%. The community college situation is more balanced, although here too men dominate with women only accounting for 37% of the faculty.

Women occupy the least secure teaching positions in higher education. They make up almost half of full-time faculty lecturers at universities, 28% of assistant professors, 15% of associate professors, and only 6% of full professors. Women are almost totally absent from senior administrative positions in post-secondary institutions. This results in women having far less influence than men on the way universities are organized and on what they teach and publish.

Women instructors are predictably better represented in "female" fields, like education, nursing, English, languages, and fine arts than they are in engineering, physics, mathematics and physiology. Women also make less money than their male colleagues at every faculty rank. Those few women who have achieved full professor status, for example, receive on average over $3000 less than their male peers. [17]

The federal employment equity program, which was legislated in 1986, applies to universities, just as it applies to all federal government contractors with at least 100 employees who bid on contracts of over $200,000. As noted in the previous chapter the programme identifies four "target groups"—women, visible minorities, native people and the disabled—whose employment prospects must be monitored. The stated aim of the programme is to eliminate policies and programs that result in employment barriers and to ensure that no one is denied employment opportunities or benefits for reasons other than lack of competence.

Canadian universities are now studying what this will mean for them. Most have employment equity officers, and are gathering systematic data on their employees in order to identify and ultimately attack employment barriers. There are no guarantees, however, that employment equity will have a major impact or that the proportion of women hired or promoted will improve substantially. In 1984 the University of Western Ontario put several new affirmative action policies into place, beginning the process even before the federal programme was initiated. In 1986 the Ontario government gave the university an Employment Equity Award. But in the first two years after this, the proportion of women faculty at Western actually dropped. In the third year there was an almost invisible improvement in the percentage of female faculty, from 14.74% to 14.78%. Recent data shows that Western is recruiting men for about two-thirds of its new appointments.[18]

The legislation of equal pay for work of equal value raises the question of comparative value, regardless of the sex of those performing the work. Quebec, Manitoba and Ontario have legislated pay equity programmes and some universities, using a variety of procedures, have begun the process of identifying and remedying pay inequities between male and female faculty.

Equal value is also a major issue for support staff and other non-academic staff in the university. For example, the union which represents the clerical, secretarial, administrative, library and technical staff at one Ontario university has recently examined pay inequities between predominantly female and predominantly male bargaining units. The starting rate for two comparable jobs in 1986 was $8.72/hour for a clerk-typist and $10.37/hour for a groundskeeper. The minimum job requirements for the clerk-typist are a grade 12 education and 2 to 4 years of experience including secretarial and/or business training. The minimum qualifications for the groundskeeper are grade 10, experience in grounds maintenance and snow removal, good physical health, and possession of a class D driver's licence. The union argued that the two jobs seemed to be at least equal regarding skill, working conditions, effort and responsibilty, yet the groundskeeper earned 19% more than the clerk-typist.[19]

Issues of employment equity and equal value are being fought at many levels—federally, provincially, on individual campuses, in trade unions, and in specific faculties and departments. These issues are also being pursued by some academic associations which have established status of women committees to examine women's positions, recommend policies and monitor them.

In contrast to post-secondary educators who teach in the very structured institutions of colleges and universities, adult educators teach in a wide variety of formal and informal settings. Research is yet to be done in Canada on the opportunities of female adult educators and the kind of power they are able to exercise in this educational sector. Impressionistic evidence suggests that as in other educational sectors, women have few opportunities and little power. Ironically, though adult education has for decades been "woman-friendly" in the sense of attracting women students as much as or more than men students, we find that men are the ones who have generally administered and organized the way adult education courses have been provided and the way that adult educators themselves are trained.

This has to change. Adult educators need to be sure that women are encouraged to apply, that the work of female teachers who teach women's subjects is valued, and that as teachers of adult students, women are consulted.

In particular, the kinds of subjects that women and men teach in adult education need to be examined for their value. No longer can we assume that women's subjects such as hobbies and crafts, personal development and general interest courses are inferior to academic or vocational courses. With a feminist analysis that stresses the standpoint of women and assesses "value" critically, the hierarchical arrangements of subjects can no longer be assumed to be natural. Rules that distinguish craft from art, hobbies from work, general interest subjects from academic, and academic from vocational need to be examined for their unchallenged assumptions and biases.

What women do can no longer be considered unimportant. As anthropologist Margaret Mead argued several decades ago: "One aspect of (the) social evaluation of different types of labour is the differentiated prestige of men's activities and women's activities. Whatever men do—even if it is dressing dolls for religious ceremonies—is more prestigious than what women do and is treated as a higher achievement." This insight applies to adult education as it does to all the other educational sectors.

We do some of our most important learning, not in formal education settings, but in our interactions with other people every day. These interactions are organized profoundly by gender, and by the ways sex and gender are implicated in the organization of families, workplaces, volunteer activities, dinner parties, friendships and leisure time—to mention just a few.

In these social relations people learn about themselves and the world they live in. The shape of these relationships affects not only how much they learn—the question of access—but also what they learn—the question of content. The fact that women are situated differently from men means that in their daily lives they learn different things from what men learn—what the baby's cries mean, who the other secretaries in the building are and what they do, where to buy panty hose and which doctors respect women. They learn how much impact they can have on others, how safe it is to voice their own opinions, and how to manipulate others when they need to. Some of this knowledge is important, some is trivial. It is all useful in some contexts and not in others. It shapes our lives profoundly. The issue of equal learning for women is not separable from the issue of equal lives.

In Conclusion

In this book we have argued that a variety of strategies is important for achieving women's educational equality. We have also argued that the strategy of "equal access" has overshadowed other strategies that are ultimately more important. Now is the time for a feminist analysis of education to be reinvigorated with more far-reaching strategies and programmes of action.

Central to a feminist analysis is the principle that women and men need to call into question the criteria which we use to value, in order to see how they have been biased in favour of men's ways of valuing, and to reshape them by taking the experiences of women into account. This revaluing is not a call to abandon judgment, nor a plea to respect just some women–those who have been good wives and mothers, or those who have achieved in male fields.

Women's experiences have to count for more by being used as a standpoint for knowledge. They have to count for more by being given greater respect and dignity and by being paid more. They have to be given equal value.

Revaluing is not just thinking women have done well. It means implementing institutional arrangements to ensure that women are paid equally and given equal authority over decision-making, that their concerns are in the curriculum, and that their knowledge is taken seriously.

Women who are members of the working classes, ethnic minority groups, and First Nations peoples have been profoundly silenced. The curriculum should help all people give voice to their experience, to analyse and understand it, and to connect it to the experience of others.

This strategy aligns feminists with other groups that are seeking to transform the curriculum and pedagogy to ensure that the working class, minority ethnic groups and other marginalized groups have a chance to value their own experiences.

This is what socialism and feminism are all about. People need to have an equal say in how their lives are organized, how power is exercised. Genuine political democracy requires economic democracy. So many groups have been left out of the consultative process. This common fate has sown the seeds of resistance. Now it is time for alliances to be formed to explore the possibilities of progressive change.

Socialist feminism provides a framework for informing such alliances. It is not an additive politics: feminism with a bit of socialism thrown in or socialism with a few concessions to women's issues. It challenges both feminism and socialism and emerges as a not uncomplicated unity of both. It is a shifting framework that emerges out of a contradictory interaction of feminism and socialism, out of a struggle to create a relation between the two. As Nancy Adamson, Linda Briskin and Margaret McPhail argue, socialist feminism privileges neither class, gender nor race as the primary source of oppression. It is "simultaneously about a transformation in the relations of domination between men and women and about a redistribution of political and economic power between classes and races."[20]

The main focus of socialist feminism is on the interconnectedness between the structures of political and economic power and the organization of male power. It assumes that the way we conduct our lives, organize our work, educate ourselves, conceive and raise our children is primarily the result of human action, not biological determinants. Exploitative relations, based on differences of class, gender, race, age or sexual orientation, are not natural, but depend on how our lives are organized economically, culturally, and politically.

Contrary to the dominant ideology of individualism in Canada, human beings are not naturally greedy, competitive and exploitative. Such traits are encouraged within the present social arrangements based on institutionalized sexism, classism and racism. This must change. Our social arrangements need to be collectively determined. With democratic social structures the potential for cooperation and caring can be fostered and the basis for a genuine alliance amongst a variety of popular movements can be built.

FOOTNOTES

[1] *Status of Women Report*, Ottawa, 1970.

[2] Neil Guppy, Doug Balson and Susan Vellutini. *Women and Higher Education in Canadian Society,* in Jane Gaskell and Arlene McLaren, **Women and Education: A Canadian Perspective.** Calgary: Detselig, 1987.

[3] For further discussion, see Guppy, et al., *Women and Higher Education in Canadian Society.*

[4] D.E. Smith et al. *A Future for Women at the University of Toronto: The Report of the Ad Hoc Committee on the Status of Women,* Centre for Women's Studies in Education, Occasional Papers, No. 13, OISE, 1985, p. 7.

[5] Provincial Access Committee, *Access to Advanced Educaiton and Job Training in British Columbia.* Victoria: Ministry of Advanced Education and Job Training, 1988.

[6] Report of the Royal Commission on the Status of Women. *Status of Women in Canada.* Ottawa: Information Canada, 1970, pp. 187-88.

[7] M..S. Devereaux. *One in Every Five: A Survey of Adult Education in Canada.* Ottawa: Minister of Supply and Services, 1985.

[8] Susan Wismer. *Women's Education and Training in Canada.* Toronto: Canadian Congress for Learning Opportunities for Women, 1988.

[9] Daniel Boothby. *Women Re-entering the Labour Force and Training Programs: Evidence from Canada, a study prepared for the Economic Council of Canada.* Ottawa: Minister of Supply and Services Canada, 1986.

[10] Dale Spender. *Learning to Create Our Own Knowledge,* **Convergence,** 13 (1-2), 1980, p. 20.

[11] D. E. Smith. *An Analysis of Ideological Structures and How Women are Excluded: Considerations for Academic Women,* pp. 241-2 in Gaskell and McLaren, **Women and Education.**

[12] T. McCormack. *Toward a Nonsexist Perspective on Social and Political Change,* pp. 11-12 in M. Mellman and R M. Kanter.. **Another Voice.** Garden City, N.Y.: Anchor Press/Doubleday, 1975.

[13] M. Eichler. **Nonsexist Research Methods: A Practical Guide.** Boston: Allen, 1988.

[14] Sandy Casey. *Status of Women.* **CAUT Bulletin,** May 1987.

[15] T. McCormack. *Feminism, Women's Studies and the New Academic Freedom* in Gaskell and McLaren. **Women and Education.**

[16] Paulo Freire. **Pedagogy of the Oppressed.** New York: The Seabury Press, 1970.

[17] See Guppy et al. *Women and Higher Education in Canadian Society.*

[18] Ann Rauhala. *Affirmative Action: A Failure, Professor at Western Reports,* **The Globe and Mail.** May 2, 1988.

[19] *Pay Equity.* **CAUT Bulletin.** December 1986, p. 10.

[20] Nancy Adamson, Linda Buskin, Margaret McPhail, *Feminist Organizng for Change: The Contemporary Women's Movement in Canada.* Toronto: Oxford Unversity Press, 1988.

JOIN THE DEBATE
ON WHAT SHOULD HAPPEN
IN CANADA'S SCHOOLS

The issues raised in books like this one will be carried on the pages of

Our Schools/Our Selves
A Magazine For Canadian Education Activists

The best way to keep in touch is to fill out of the subscription forms at the back and mail it in.

But we hope you'll do more than read us. We hope you'll get involved in these issues, if you aren't already.
And that you'll let us know what you think of our articles and books.

FOR A YEAR'S SUBSCRIPTION YOU'LL GET
4 MAGAZINES AND 4 BOOKS.

The next issue of the magazine (November 1989) will include articles on:

Mulroney's Corporate Education Initiative — Private School Funding — Racism and Aids Education in Nova Scotia Schools — Education in Mozambique — Privatizing our College System — Peace Activism in Quebec Schools — Children of the State, Part II — School Consolidation in P.E.I. — Workers and the Rise of Mass Schooling — The Manitoba High School Review — Trading-in Saskatchewan's Trade Schools — The Politics of Standard English — High Schools and Teen Age Sex — The New Political Agenda in B.C. Education.

IN THE FIRST THREE YEARS OF
OUR SCHOOLS/OUR SELVES
YOU WILL HAVE RECEIVED THE FOLLOWING BOOKS:

- Ken Osborne, **Educating Citizens: A Democratic Socialist Agenda for Canadian Education**
- La Maîtresse d'école, **Building a People's Curriculum: The Experience of a Quebec Teachers' Collective**
- Jane Gaskell, Arlene McLaren, Myra Novogrodsky, **Claiming an Education: Feminism and Canadian Schools**
- Jim Turk, ed., **Labour, Education, and Skill Training**
- Jim Cummins, Marcel Danesi, **The Development and Denial of Canada's Linguistic Resources**
- Loren Lind, **Their Rightful Place: The Childcare Issue in Canada**
- Célestin Freinet, **Techniques of Cooperative Learning**
- Ken Osborne, **The Politics of Teaching: A Democratic Socialist Approach to Pedagogy in Canadian Schools**
- Bruce Kidd, **Kids, Sports, and the Body: A Feminist Socialist Approach to Physical Education**
- William Bruneau, David Clandfield, **Where Does The NDP Stand in Education?**
- Doug Noble, **The Military/Corporate Agenda in North American Education**
- Celia Haig-Brown, Robert Regnier, ed., **A Strategy for Native Education in Canada**

The subscription price for each of these books will be as much as 50% off the bookstore price.

Subscribe Today And Give
A Subscription Form To A Friend